MW01031233

Fallen Angels

Giants, UFO Encounters & The New World Order

CK Quarterman

FALLEN ANGELS

CK QUARTERMAN

Giants, UFO Encounters & The New World Order

AMBASSADOR INTERNATIONAL
GREENVILLE, SOUTH CAROLINA & BELFAST, NORTHERN IRELAND

www.ambassador-international.com

Fallen Angels
Giants, UFO Encounters & The New World Order

Printed in the United States of America

ISBN: 9781935507895
eISBN: 9781935507994

Unless otherwise indicated all Scripture quotations are taken from KJV

Cover Design & Page Layout David Siglin

AMBASSADOR INTERNATIONAL
Emerald House
427 Wade Hampton Blvd.
Greenville, SC 29609, USA
www.ambassador-international.com

AMBASSADOR BOOKS
The Mount
2 Woodstock Link
Belfast, BT6 8DD, Northern Ireland, UK
www.ambassador-international.com

The colophon is a trademark of Ambassador

Contents

Acknowledgments

This book would not have been possible without the support of my friends Tracy Hodgson, Dr. Bob Schnakenberg, and my dear wife, Beth. I want to extend special thanks in memory of my loving auntie, Rosalie Cowart, who taught me that loving everyone is possible. To my readers who honor me for taking the time out of their busy lives to read this book, I thank you.

A GREAT LIGHT

Out of confusion and despair,
A great light hath shone
To calm the tempest blown
For surely I am the Lord,
No greater God be known,
For there is none beside me
For I am alone, only I can atone.

As far as the heavens are above
The earth, I have made my Word known.
No longer am I unknown, but shown,
For I have sent One to atone.
I am known from the groan
Of the frigid zone to Sierra Leone.

I am the builder's stone to break the bone
That you might pass the stone and be fully Grown.
For this time is a passing zone
Not to be fully shown, but unknown.
Be of good cheer and make known
How you are shown, and you shall not be alone.
I shall be by your side, and I shall not disown.

CK Quarterman

PROLOGUE

In a time of universal deceit-telling the truth is a revolutionary act.

—George Orwell

SOME PEOPLE ARE GOING TO need to be convinced; they are going to need more than the Sunday sermon because they are sincerely grappling with misconceptions of safety and peace that need to be dealt with. These misconceptions are like roadblocks in front of them that must be removed so they can advance and embrace the truth of the hour in which we live.

A time similar to that which Winston Churchill faced during the dark, prewar years also faces us. We have a short time to blow the trumpet, to make people aware that the Four Horsemen of the Apocalypse are about to begin their ride. We, like Churchill, must not give ourselves over to appeasing men. We must bellow the warning from the roof tops, in the highways and byways. It's time to be no longer politically correct, no matter the price. We must warn those in darkness, regardless of the cost to ourselves personally!

Winston Churchill maintained a strong attack on appeasement with the Nazis; he never considered the cost too high. He railed at Great Britain's legislative body's failure to stand up to Nazi tyranny. Churchill spoke out continually against appeasement. After the occupation of Austria, Churchill spoke in Parliament saying, "For five years I have talked to the House on these matters, not with very great success. I have watched this famous island descending incontinently, fecklessly, the stairway which leads to a dark gulf. It is a fine broad stairway at the beginning, but after a bit the carpet ends. A little farther on, there are only flag stones; a little farther on still, these flag stones break beneath your feet.

That it is asleep none might argue. The world must put off its slumber and prepare to expose the darkness which soon will overtake it.

"If mortal catastrophe should overtake the British nation, historians a thousand years hence will never understand how it was that the victorious nation suffered themselves to cast away all that they had gained by measureless sacrifice. Now the victors are vanquished, and those who threw down their arms are striding on to world mastery."

Upon Chamberlin's return from Munich and his "I bring you peace, peace in our time" speech, Churchill stood up in the House of Commons and gave this speech.

"I do not grudge our loyal, brave people the spontaneous outburst of joy, but they should know the truth. They should know that we have sustained a defeat without war. And do not suppose that this is the end. This is only the beginning, the first sip, the first foretaste of the bitter cup which will be proffered to us year by year unless, by a supreme recovery of moral health and military vigor, we arise again and take our stand for freedom as in the olden times."

This was not what Parliament or the English people wanted to hear; they jeered, rejected, and spoke badly of Churchill, accusing him of being a warmonger.

And ye shall be hated of all men for my name's sake (Matt. 10:22).

I have written this work solely for the purpose of awakening the world from its slumber. That it is asleep none might argue. The world must put off its slumber and prepare to expose the darkness which soon will overtake it.[1]

The politically correct have begun to seek peace and safety at the cost of morally correct stances. This peace and safety can only be temporary, for peace and safety shall elude the world. The world is in a slumber, hoping for a better tomorrow.

At the pinnacle of the conspiratorial hierarchy is a distinct, malevolent, eternal, and all powerful evil force manipulating lesser conspiratorial actors.

Citing source data is the scientific method of research, but citing source data does not seem to apply to so-called "conspiracy theories." A thousand sources may be quoted, yet it will not convince the skeptics of the truth. It seems something sinister is working behind the panorama that does not want you to know the truth. Remember, the truth is out there (quoting X Files). Refusing to see does not mean that one cannot see; it just means one refuses to see.

The end is near, America is failing, and the footfall of the Four Horsemen of the Apocalypse is on the doorstep. In order to prove that most Americans are willfully blind to what's happening around them, I created a survey, and I am going to share with you the results.

In this survey, I asked several questions at random to Facebook fans of all age groups. I conducted this survey in the blind without asking for personally indentifying information. One question that I asked was "while in a busy mall, you walk past a person sitting on a bench talking to a cardboard dog. What would you do?"

True to what I expected, most people when asked to answer this survey question answered it by saying they would ignore the person. What does this say about Americans? I think it says Americans prefer to ignore the obvious if it in any way makes them feel uncomfortable.

The correct response would be to allow curiosity to inspire questions. Curiosity could be rewarded with questions such as "what is this? Why is a man talking to a cardboard dog? Is it really a cardboard dog? Could this cardboard dog be a prototype robot? Is this the chance of a lifetime for a spot on television's Candid Camera?"

The strange and possibly supernatural should inspire us to ask questions that beg answers. It is in this way that we learn truth.

The great discoveries of this century have been made due to curiosity. A good example of this is penicillin, which was discovered when someone asked himself a question about a mold. Curiosity spawns questions that when answered make our lives easier here in the 21st century.

Within these pages, you may find your own cardboard dog. It may be a preconceived idea, a reaction, a previously unheard of explanation, or the use of historical works such as the Book of Enoch and the Book of Jubilees. I view these books as historical writings on the same level as the writings of Flavius Josephus and Julius Caesar but not on the level of inspired Scripture. This use of historical works could be someone's cardboard dog; don't let it be yours. Let this book inspire your curiosity regardless of your discomfort.

Another survey question asked, "will the future be a better day for your children; will they have a better life than yourself?" Over half the respondents answered "yes," they believed that their children's future would be a better day and that their children would lead better lives.

Perhaps this would be true–if not for the fallen angels, if not for the fact that the Book of the Apocalypse speaks of worsening times and of a time of judgment upon the inhabitants of the earth. But this is nothing new!

Mankind has always deceived itself.

Most people think of themselves as individualists, as people who come to a conclusion based upon sound reason and the facts they are given, not because they are simply following other people or another person's opinion. Most people see themselves as leaders when in fact they are followers. The sad fact is that history has shown that people have a herd mentality. People prefer to follow one another like cattle.

> **The forces arrayed against us have never been greater, nor the threats more real. It is in this dark hour that we must make our stand.**

A herd mentality can be seen in beliefs propagated by today's gurus–beliefs such as "the market will resume its upward march, thereby rewarding all those who have kept the faith," "real estate is always a good investment," "real estate will always keep gaining value," and "invest in stocks for the long run." All such beliefs prove people are followers; in the face of contrary facts, it proves even further that they are not only followers but are participating in a mass delusion. Mass delusion has become the national norm. People want to believe politicians, think that things will always work out right in the long run, and hope that the economy is going to get better. People want to believe what they hear on television. They want to be told by the "experts" and "gurus" how to live and what to believe. They want assurance that no matter how they live or what they do, there will be no repercussions. Being uncritical and non-judgmental is the unspoken norm, and to oppose someone's manner of life, his beliefs, or his relationships is to be politically incorrect. The fact is that it has now become illegal to voice an opposition to someone's manner of life, and it is now called a hate crime.

How will the world hear and[2] prepare if not warned? Churchill faced this problem, but he persevered, speaking to anyone who would listen, making many enemies and sabotaging his career. But, he had a love of truth and spoke about things as he saw them.

Truth must be sought. First and foremost, truth must be sought, apprehended, and cuddled tightly to the chest like a childhood toy. Held tightly and refused to be let go. Truth must dwell in an open mind, not one closed by political correctness.

Many of us presume to know truth, but in reality we do not.[3] Truth is hidden! Truth must be searched out; it must be sought as a[4] pearl. Truth must be found, but it is not found easily.[5]

A misunderstanding of truth is the norm because ignorance is a chosen response. When our leaders, parents, teachers, and even pastors have believed a lie, we must allow our minds and hearts to be especially open in order to see. When our role models have believed a lie, the truth might be right out in the open for us to see for ourselves. However, too often we fail to see it, intent upon seeing only what we expect to see.

Truth and[6] wisdom are personified in Proverbs.

The "fear of the LORD is the beginning of knowledge" (Prov. 1:7). The Lord says "Pride goes before destruction, a haughty spirit before a fall" (Prov. 16:18). Haughtiness leads to an inability to recognize truth. Could America today be haughty?

The forces arrayed against us have never been greater, nor the threats more real. It is in this dark hour that we must make our stand.

The truth must be told as never before, the just must speak out and persuade the wavering and the unbeliever.

But they are going to need more than proclamation; they will need the utter truth. Not the lukewarm ear-tickling of times past, but the bloodcurdling truth!

It must be in this last hour that we overcome the fallen angels by speaking the truth—no, not by speaking the truth alone, but by proclaiming it in the face of the scoffer, the hater, and the bully; if necessary, even speaking the truth at the risk of our lives.

Government is not won over by the well meaning; the well meaning don't change society or even make better citizens.

When we should have been seeking the truth, we were out trying to change the world through politics. We have presumed to persuade others to party affiliation instead of from unbelief to belief. The world must awake from its slumber, put off its lukewarm manners, and prepare for battle. The trumpet is now beginning to sound…

THE
NEPHILIM

But as the days of Noah were, so shall also the coming of the Son of man be

— Matt. 24:37 (KJV)

On earth there once were giants.

— Greek Poet Homer (400BC)

THE WORD NEPHILIM APPEARS IN the Bible twice: once in Genesis and again in Numbers. The definition of nephilim is the offspring of the "sons of God" and the "daughters of men" as well as the giants who inhabited Canaan before the Israelites. We know that the "sons of God" are fallen angels. The "daughters of men" are human women. The two should not have been coming together, but clearly they were, and the result of such unions were beings known as nephilim, larger and stronger than mere human beings.

> *And God looked upon the earth, and, behold, it was cor-*
> *rupt; for all flesh had corrupted his way upon the earth*
> (Gen. 6:12) (KJV).

So as happened in the days of Noah, we might see these nephilim today, and they may or may not look human! Remember the Egyptian symbols called hieroglyphs seen on ancient artifacts? They depicted half-human, half-animal creatures. Could these cultures actually have seen these creatures and drawn depictions of what they saw? I think so. In fact, I believe I've seen one myself! But I'm getting ahead of myself. That's not the beginning of the story, and the beginning is where we must start to make sense of it all.

THE UNSEEN BATTLE

WE NEED TO ASK SOME very serious questions and demand some very serious answers.

These are the last moments of time, and we don't have the luxury of sitting on the pew any longer! It's time to suit up for the battle.

The story I will tell you will be a long one, it will course through eons and ages of time, but it will bring Lucifer, fallen angels, and the conspiracy to light as God's forces bring them to justice.

Lucifer has worked hard to keep this part of history hidden, but in this chapter I will attempt to explain how Lucifer and the fallen angels have effected humanity and poisoned its genetic code, how at times he and his cohorts have almost won, and how the Heavenly Host was able to hold back the tide; even now, the Host is pushing the tide back. God's Host (angels) have been doing battle since almost the beginning of time. Lucifer and fallen angels are among us, unknown by us, and I believe it has been determined that it is now time to come out of hiding.

They have hidden among mankind, appearing very similar to ourselves. But, they are very different. Their DNA has never been studied, and their DNA has never been seen. Their creations, the nephilim, have been studied, of course, but they themselves have not. They have eluded capture and justice and are the vilest of beings, but they can appear charming.

Fallen angels are eternal and therefore must reinvent themselves every generation or risk exposure.

You are familiar with some of their names. They appear out of nowhere in history. They have no descendants, no genealogy.

Fallen angels are eternal and therefore must reinvent themselves every generation or risk exposure. They operate very much as the fictional characters of the popular television series Highlander. The premise of the series is that the Highlanders must, every generation, disappear and reinvent themselves somewhere else in order not to call attention to the fact that they don't age, for if it were revealed that they didn't age, their game would be up. Thus, Lucifer and his cohorts, the fallen angels, have to operate similarly in order to avoid detection.

They use trusts and shadow corporations to maintain a vast amount of wealth, and therefore they remain the rulers and power brokers of mankind in every generation.

Other television series mimic the same theme but with a science fiction twist. Programs such as V, The Event, The X-files, and many others have had the same foundational theme of conspirators behind the scenes pulling strings.

Many of these television series have dealt with a plot of a hidden alien invasion overseen by elements of corrupt government and mysterious international "syndicates."

The Illuminati and Bilderbergs of common folklore pale in comparison to the real conspiracy and the real conspirators. This Lucifer and his fallen angels are the master manipulators behind the picture of time; they are the string pullers and the puppet masters. Shakespeare may have caught a glimpse of this unseen war when he wrote that men are merely actors upon a stage. Truer words may never have been spoken!

> **Do not be afraid and do not be dismayed at this great horde, for the battle is not yours but God's**

It is now that I know the battle may be won, but the war lost. I now see as through a general's eyes that the victory isn't always to the[7] strong or the outcome of battle assured by a general's wise tactics. Man decides neither the battle nor the outcome of war. Battles are thought to be fought between men and their ideologies, with one side or the other claiming the victory. This is not the case; battles are fought and the outcomes determined by forces unseen to the naked eye.

Do not be afraid and do not be dismayed at this great horde, for the battle is not yours but God's (2 Chronicles 20:15).

Dark and sinister forces vie for the outcome of battles. These dark forces are much more evil than the measure of evil in man and are only held at bay by the power of the Lord's Host (angels). It is these sinister and dark forces with which humanity strives and that must be conquered. These unseen forces are for the most part hidden from the mortal eye. Lucifer and the fallen angels have watched and intervened in humanity since the dawn of time.

Occasionally, the[8] unseen battle might be glimpsed, as happened with[9] the Emperor Constantine in[10] AD 312 at the Battle of the

Milvian Bridge, or such a glimpse as happened at the Battle of the Mons in 1914.

In August of 1914, near Mons in Belgium, the first British and German forces encountered each other in WWI. The British Expeditionary Force came under vastly superior German fire in the opening stages of the battle. Heavily outnumbered, their demise seemed certain. But the British, outnumbered approximately four to one, were saved at the last moment by a brigade of warrior angels that wrought destruction upon the Germans, handing the victory

Do not be afraid and do not be dismayed at this great horde, for the battle is not yours but God's

to the British; however, they suffered heavy casualties and were outflanked and forced to retreat the next day.

Comparable accounts of such battlefield visions have occurred in ancient and medieval warfare. These famous episodes were interventions by unseen forces. In these cases it was the Army of the Lord (angels) that was glimpsed.

The prophet Daniel attested to this unseen battle when he wrote,[11] "And I lifted up mine eyes, and looked, and behold a man clothed in linen and girded about with gold, whose face was like the appearance of lightning, and his eyes were as lamps of fire, and his arms and his legs looked like shining brass, and the voice of his words were as the voice of a multitude. One like the resemblance of the sons of men, an Angel said to me, 'O Daniel; understand that which I speak, for I have been sent to you from the first day that you prayed. I have come because of your prayer. But the Dark Lord, the prince of the kingdom of the Persians, withstood me until Michael, a chief prince, came to help me'" (paraphrased).

The prince of the Persians was a fallen angel who withstood the angel who was sent to speak to Daniel.

One caution: this conspiracy is neither limited by humanity's awareness of it nor by lack of humanity's ability to grasp it. As I write this, I wonder why I must bring this message. Why must I, out of the vast, undulating mass of humanity, tell this message? Are there not others willing to pay a price?

The prince of the Persians was a fallen angel who withstood the angel who was sent to speak to Daniel.

It's not that I haven't desired to tell this message, for I have. It's not that I haven't paid a price, for I have. It's not that I haven't been attacked upon every turn, both by seen and unseen forces, for I have! Still I press forward, determined to spread the word and sound the alarm.

TIME BEFORE TIME

What was before nothingness?

GOD EXISTED. I REMEMBERED SUDDENLY, like a bolt of lightning, Genesis 1:1. *In the beginning God.*

Before anything was, there was God, and then he created the heavens and earth. Before nothingness, there was God.

I will start our discussion with a time in the [12]eons past when nothing existed but[13] God.

It is important to understand the players in the game in order to understand the conspiracy.

We will use the analogy of chess. God is the king piece. The captain of the Lord's Host (Jesus) is the knight, and the heavenly host is represented by the pawns. The bishop piece represents the righteous ones, and the board is the stage of life.

The opposing side has as its king, Lucifer. The knight is Beelzebub, and the bishop piece represents the unrighteous ones.

The pawns are the fallen angels. Humanity is stuck in no man's land between the opposing forces, merely, as Shakespeare said, being actors upon the stage of the chess game of life.

> **It is important to understand the players in the game in order to understand the conspiracy.**

The time, in the beginning before anything, before even the earth was created, a time before the heavens were prepared, a time referred to as[14] "from everlasting," a time when the cosmos and its laws of gravitation, diminishing return, and matter were not in existence. This is the time in which this game began to be played.

In order to grasp the concept of "from everlasting," one must grasp the time and place of its beginning. God called into existence the space-time realm; there was no time before creation. Time is something that is exclusive to this realm in which we live. The Ancient of Days exists outside time and space in eternity. Time was created along with the other realms and beings and began at a finite point out of nonexistence.

To the casual observer, the moment of creation might appear as a singularity or a big bang.

This singularity was the result of having the realms compressed into two words which the Lord spoke. When God spoke the words "Light be," these words exploded into the worlds we see now, the realms we don't see, and the rudiments and stones of fire. Neither shadow nor illumination existed before creation. The Lord made this physical realm by mere[15] will of having it appear, without any use of preexistent substance. Theologians refer to this as creatio ex nihilo, meaning "creation out of nothing." There are dimensions of reality without number and dimensions that cannot be calculated. The realms were created out of the very substance and nature of God. We are all in this manner His children because of this creative act. We had preexistence within the mind of God.

The Lord lives in a realm which has no beginning and no end, and because He is in a timeless present, His perspective sees our past, present, and future as a present happening.

He is, therefore, uniquely positioned to judge all things because He sees what is happening everywhere in the different realms at any time, whether in history present, past, or future.

There are many dimensions, some of which exist alongside this dimension.

Many people are incapable of imagining other dimensions. But these dimensions are real nevertheless. A person cannot detect these other dimensions with their senses. However, mathematicians are beginning to understand because one way to think about other dimensions is to think in terms of circles which curl upon themselves and intertwine with time.

The things seen and unseen consist of more than the few dimensions we are aware of. There are no fewer than ten dimensions, but I cannot describe what they look like or how you might approach an understanding of them. But suffice it to say they are beautiful and full of wonder!

I can tell you this: one day humanity will transverse these dimensions, not at what we would call the speed of light, but faster, at the speed of thought.

This will be during the time of restoration of all things in heaven and earth.

Let's look at how angels travel, for this will be important later; they simply *will* themselves to be somewhere, and they are there. They have no sense of traveling, no sense of boundaries; there are no walls to impede their movement.

Let me offer a simple explanation: an angel can be at any moment in the center of a circle or move in any direction and remain equidistant to every point around the circle's circumference at any given moment of time.

God and Jesus were in the beginning before "nothingness." Jesus created all things. Jesus is not a created being but was in existence with God before there was even an everlasting. *Logos* is Greek for *expression* or *utterance* and is defined by the passage itself in the fourteenth verse to be Jesus.

> *In the beginning was the Word (Logos-Jesus), and the Word was with God, and the Word was God. The same was in the beginning with God. All things were made by him (the Logos-Jesus); and without him was not any thing made that was made (John 1:1–3).*

The evil players in the chess game of life are Lucifer and the fallen angels who themselves *are* created beings, who were not in existence from everlasting.

Lucifer and the fallen angels are relative new comers to the game, having been introduced merely 3.8 to 4.1 billion years ago (my estimate of the time of Lucifer's fall).[16]

Jesus has intervened many times on mankind's behalf and indeed is the architect of mankind.

All things are[17] held together by the Word (Logos–Jesus). Every part of creation affects every other part of creation, and all creation is[18] framed by the word of God (Logos–Jesus) so that things which are seen were not made of things which do appear.

Only a small record of this time is left to us in the Hebrew Old Testament. It seems likely that most of the records have been destroyed by Lucifer and the fallen angels in order to conceal themselves, but in the[19] oldest of writings, there is some record of this time and the events which took place.

Imagine, if you can, twenty-four elders sitting upon thrones, and in the center a larger throne, with the host (angels) in attendance as witnesses. The congregation is unnumbered because of the multitudes in attendance.

This meeting is sometimes referred to as the Divine Council,[20] and it was mentioned several times in the Old Testament where it was referred to as the Congregation (assembly).

Seated upon[21] the center throne was the Lord. The throne was made of jasper and rubies that caused a rainbow to encircle the throne. The elders around the larger throne wore white robes, and on their heads were crowns of gold, and from the larger throne crackled thunderous voices like lightening.

A crystal sea of glass sparkled in the light of seven torches. Four living beings stood sentinel around the center throne.

The first was like a lion. The second was like a calf. The third had the face of a man, and the fourth was like an eagle. Each had six wings and were full of eyes around and within.[22] Before the throne was a golden altar.

Concerning this Council, we are told the following story in the Hebrew Old Testament.[23]

> And the Lord said, "Who shall entice this king that he may go and be defeated at Ramoth Gilead?" And one said on this manner; and another said on that manner. And there came forth another, and stood before the Lord, and said, "I will convince him." And the Lord said to him, "Wherewith?" And he said, "I will go, and will be a lying spirit in the mouth of all his prophets."

And he said, "You will convince him, go now, and do so" [24] *and one said, on that manner and another (1 Kings 22).*

There was a low whisper heard as the members of the counsel began to raise their voices in agreement as the lying spirit left.

The lying spirit enticed the king to disobey God, and the king was slain in battle at Ramoth Gilead.

So we see that before this Divine Council, both good and bad were represented.

Now there was a day when the **sons of God** *(beney 'elohim) came to present themselves before the LORD, and* **Satan** *came also among them. And the LORD said unto Satan, Whence comest thou? Then Satan answered the LORD, and said, From going to and fro in the earth, and from walking up and down in it (Job 1:6–7).*

We know from the Book of Job that the fallen angels and Satan addressed this Council. Satan negotiated before the Council for Job. God spoke for the Council but allowed Job to be afflicted, only sparing his life.

So in this time before time began, which we refer to as from everlasting to everlasting, there was God, Jesus (Word –Logos), and they were sitting at the head of the Council with the twenty-four elders and the Congregation before them. What a picture!

HOW THE CONSPIRACY BEGAN

The conspiracy had its beginning in Lucifer the Dark Prince.

HE WASN'T ALWAYS DARK. HE became evil of his own choosing. Lucifer ruled over the vast realms of creation, but Lucifer was condemned for his attempt to take over the throne of God. Those who were with him then and those who followed him later are now referred to as fallen angels, or sometimes the Dark Lords of Rahab. The name Rahab comes from what was once Lucifer's planet and home before its destruction.

Now have you ever wondered what would make some being have this motivation? Why would a being of a heavenly realm be motivated to rebel against God? What was he trying to gain?

Many eons ago, on the planet Rahab, evil was birthed in the heart of its ruler, Lucifer. The Dark Prince ruled and controlled the many spiritual and physical realms from a stone of fire (planet) called Rahab. This evil is commonly known as pride, but a much more malevolent emotion was lurking under the surface of pride. Put simply, the sin of pride is trouble enough, but back-stabbing[25] greed lurked beneath Lucifer's pride.

Before Lucifer the Dark Prince rebelled, there was trade between the planets (stones of fire), solar systems, and universes.[26]

He didn't just rule over the stones of fire but also interplanetary trade. Rahab was once a planet like ours, orbiting the sun. It was larger than the Earth, more along the lines of Saturn. Its name means boaster or pride because its mass could hold ten Earths. Its orbit was nearly circular. Now all that remains of Rahab is the asteroid belt.[27] Before, like Mars, it was once inhabited with many wonderful beings of the spiritual realm. Unlike Mars, the Lord's host destroyed Rahab. [28] Mars, a once-beautiful stone of fire, had its atmosphere stripped away.

The Dark Prince was mad with fury, flinging fire from the sky, raining down his terror and destruction, but to no avail. The Ancient of Days watched as his beautiful, prideful, greedy creation stormed across universes, thunderously out of control. Lucifer hurled accusation after accusation and shook with anger until he was without speech and his anger had turned to fear. Then God's whisper was heard.

1 Every wonderful planet was in your control, the sardius (Mercury), topaz (Venus), and the diamond (Mars), the beryl (Earth), the onyx (Saturn), and the jasper (Jupiter), the sapphire (Rahab), the emerald (Neptune), and the carbuncle (Uranus), and gold (Pluto). The deputyship of your mode of movement in the physical realm (think noise of exhaust pipes) was prepared in you in the day that I created you.

You were the anointed Prince over the entire realm, and I placed you in this lofty position. You freely traveled through the stones of fire, the solar systems, and the universes.

You were perfect in your ways from the day you were created until this rebellion came into you. But the massive amount of your trade and the position of rule you held over all has filled you with greed and violence. You have decided in your heart to take from Me what I have not given you (Ezekiel 28:13 paraphrased).

This mentality of back-stabbing greed is common among men, where it is called the[29] "mafia mentality. It is the consciousness of one's own worth, the exaggerated concept of individual force as the sole arbitrator of every conflict, of every clash of interests or ideas. Lucifer, desiring to extend his personal rule beyond that which was given to him, fell into this mafia mentality, desiring to reach beyond the stars to rule all the material and spiritual realms himself!

It is important to remember that there were others watching. The[30] Congregation watched this rebellion taking place.

They observed this drama being played out with great interest. They witnessed the Prince of Rahab (Lucifer) stand up in the assembly and rebel.

---

[1]   *Thou hast been in Eden the garden of God; every precious stone was thy covering, the sardius, topaz, and the diamond, the beryl, the onyx, and the jasper, the sapphire, the emerald, and the carbuncle, and gold: the workmanship of thy tabrets and of thy pipes was prepared in thee in the day that thou wast created* (Ezekiel 28:13 KJV).

There had never been a revolt. No one had ever thought to raise up against the creator, the Lord.

The assembly observed the Prince's bid for a greater piece of the pie. Then the Lord said,

So I cast you, defiled one, from the height of the realm, and I will destroy you from among the stones of fire. Your heart became greedy because of your great position and beauty; you corrupted the wisdom I had given you because of your high and exalted position. I therefore cast you from heaven to the earth (Ezekiel 28:14–17 paraphrased).

> **Woe unto the inhabitants of the earth, for with great fury is he cast down.**

They watched in shock as the Dark Prince gathered false courage. Because of the audience, he dared not back away.

They all watched, thinking Lucifer would become extinct in the next few breaths; instead, God raised his eyes, as if composing what he would say, but none dared to meet his gaze.

He spoke. *Thou art cast out from heaven, O Lucifer, you the shining one! You are cut down to the ground!*

Upon hearing this, Lucifer hardened his heart against God, and he began immediately to take up arms against God. Some of the others were so bold as to join in the fight alongside the Prince of Rahab.

They were cast out of heaven and became known as the fallen angels or Dark Lords. Here upon the Earth, the battle festers as a wound which refuses to be closed.

Woe unto the inhabitants of the earth, for with great fury is he cast down (Rev. 12:12).

And fight he has, first in the spiritual realm and now in the physical.

DESOLATE PLANET

The annihilation of Lucifer's home, Rahab, isn't in the shared conscious-ness or memory of humanity. It happened long before the first of our race was created!

BUT AGAINST ALL THE EFFORT of the fallen angels to suppress this information, there remains this one record, that of the lost Book of Enoch. We must accept it not as canon but as a historical book in its own right. The Book of Enoch is mentioned in the Bible.

And Enoch also, the seventh from Adam, prophesied of these, saying, "Behold, the Lord cometh with ten thousands of his saints" (Jude 1:14).

The Book of Enoch almost made it into the canon. Some believe had it not been for its detail concerning fallen angels and giants, it would have been accepted into the canon.

I hold the Book of Enoch and the Book of Jubilees in high regard as to their historical authenticity. These books do not contradict the Scripture in the least but do, however, give more detail concerning subjects such as fallen angels and giants. So going forward, we will use the Old and New Testaments, the Book of Enoch, and the Book of Jubilees to expound upon our subject. However, before coming to the present, we must go back in time to Earth's earliest beginnings.

> **I hold the Book of Enoch and the Book of Jubilees in high regard as to their historical authenticity.**

God created the Earth in Genesis 1:1 but destroyed the Earth by the second verse of Genesis. This belief is based on the second verse's statement that the Earth was without form and void.

> *And the earth was without form, and void; and darkness was upon the face of the deep. And the Spirit of God moved upon the face of the waters (Gen. 1:2).*

I like the way the Message Bible says it,

Earth was a soup of nothingness, a bottomless emptiness, an inky blackness (Gen. 1:2).[31]

Before the six days of Genesis, the Earth was a dead, desolate planet, drifting in the freezing frozen night of space.[32]

Earth is underwater and is an uninhabited[33] stone of fire (planet), wandering in the cold and dark remains of an old creation. The land is submerged, and the water's angry wrath abounds. Abyss calls unto abyss. The lonely night gets ever darker, ever longing for the dawn that doesn't appear. Earth was a lifeless chunk of rock, hurrying through the cosmos with no sun to warm its waters or touch its lifeless mass. The planet had drifted off its axis, and was being bombarded with asteroid after asteroid!

Rahab's judgment has taken place. We will later call this time the[2] Late Heavy Bombardment Period.

About 3.8 to 4.1 billion years ago, these asteroids that had made up the core of the stone of fire called Rahab impacted the Earth.

These asteroids caused great destruction. Our moon, Mercury, Venus, and Mars were bombarded without mercy. Our solar system was damaged beyond any self-repair. Earth alone received 22,000 impact craters, and several craters had diameters larger than 5,000 miles. What we now know as the Caribbean Sea is in actuality an impact crater from this time. It was by means of these great rocks of Rahab that Earth became a formless void and the solar system damaged.

With Lucifer's and the fallen angels' rebellion, death and corruption began to invade the stones of fire, and this dimension, which was under the Dark Lord's rule, was judged, and the whole of the cosmos and all things in it began to decay.

Because he was the prince of this physical cosmos, all things under his rule were subjected to corruption and death.

The stones of fire beneath his control had the judgment of death and corruption pronounced upon them, and they were subjected to casualty, vice, and eventual death.

_____

[2]   The Late Heavy Bombardment is a period of time approximately 4.1 to 3.8 billion years ago during which a large number of impact craters were formed on the moon, and by inference on Earth, Mercury, Venus, and Mars as well. The evidence for this event comes from the dating of lunar samples, which indicates that most impact rocks formed in this rather narrow interval of time. Extrapolating lunar cratering rates to Earth at this time suggest the following: 22,000 or more impact craters with diameters of more than 20 miles, about 40 impact basins with diameters about 1000 miles, several impact basins with diameters about 5,000 miles, such as the Caribbean . From Wikipedia, The Geological Society, Space.com

The prophet Jeremiah spoke of this time.

[34] I looked upon the earth, and it was underwater, and uninhabited; I saw no light. The mountains and hills trembled, and moved ever so slightly. I considered, and, lo, there was no man, and no birds or animals of any kind. I looked even harder and the vineyards were destroyed, and all the cities were wrecked by the anger of the Lord. The whole world was deserted; there was no population (Jer. 4:23).

I hold the Book of Enoch and the Book of Jubilees in high regard as to their historical authenticity.

What civilizations were upon this Earth vanished beneath the roaring and swirling waves. A planet covered in water without light. The world as we now know it sprung from this wasteland.

The [35] six days of Genesis are an account of a [36]re-creation of a previously existing creation, not the original creation of the Earth.

God created the two great lights, the greater light (the sun) for regulating the day and the lesser light (the moon) for regulating the night.

He appointed the greater light to shine upon all the Earth and to rule over the day.

And He divided the light from the darkness that all things might flourish in their time upon the Earth.

He created the firmament in the midst of the waters and divided the firmament between the water that was under the firmament and the water that was above the firmament. He commanded the waters to pass from off the face of the Earth into one place and the dry land to appear. On that day, He created all the rivers and lakes. He created the seed that is sown, the fruit bearing trees, and all sprouting plants, each according to its kind and likeness.

These great works did the Lord, and the Host saw His works.

He created the great whales in the depths of the abyss, everything that moves in the sea, and everything that flies. He created all the animals of the earth and everything that moves upon the earth.

These great works did the Lord, and the Host saw His works.

The Lord said, "Let us make man according to our image and according to our likeness."

And the Lord made man according to His image. In the image of the Lord, he made man.

Adam was not created in the garden of Eden. He was created from the clay of Canaan and put into the garden.

*And the LORD God planted a garden eastward in Eden; and **there he put the man whom he had formed*** (Gen. 2:8).

The Hebrew root word for dust is clay, which derives its meaning, *ruddy*, from the reddish tint that gives clay its color. It is also the root word for Canaan. Adam was made from the dust or, if you will, the clay of Canaan land. Adam was made from the clay of what would later be known as the Temple Mount.

The Lord created the Garden of Delight in the east of the Earth towards the rising sun, a place beautifully planted with all manner of trees and filled with brilliant, dazzling scenery. And the Lord made to spring up every tree stunning to the gaze and superior for food, and He also placed there a tree of learning the knowledge of good and evil.

To the north of the garden, He created a river of water, clear and pure to the taste, unlike anything else; it proceeded from the depths of the Earth and from the root of the Tree of Life, and it encircled the whole land of the Garden of Delight where there was gold, sapphire, and emerald. It divided itself into the rivers Geon, Tigris, and Euphrates.

The Garden of Delight was created to shield and protect Adam from the world around him that had been subjected to sin and corruption by the fallen angels. Although the world had been remade after its destruction, it was still subjected to Lucifer.

The Lord blessed Adam, telling him to increase and multiply and refill the earth and subdue it. And the Lord gave Adam dominion over everything that moved on the earth, in the abyss, and over everything that flew.

These great works did the Lord, and the Host saw His works.

The Lord said, "It is not good that man should be alone, let us make for him a help meet."

The Host brought unto Adam all the beasts, and everything that moved on the Earth, according to its kind, and Adam named them all by their individual names. As Adam called them, so became their name. Adam saw all the beasts, according to their kind, but he found no help meet for himself in these beasts. So the Lord caused a deep slumber to fall upon Adam, and He took one rib from among Adam's ribs, and from this rib He created the woman, that she might be a help meet for him.

After having created woman, God then awakened Adam out of his deep slumber. Upon Adam's awaking, He brought the woman to him.

Adam knew her and said, "This is now bone of my bone and flesh of my flesh. She shall be called Woman, because she was taken out of Man."

Adam called the name of his wife Eve, because she was the mother of all living. Both Adam and Eve were given bodies of a very bright nature.

These great works did the Lord, and the Host saw His works.

Adam and his wife were in the Garden of Delight keeping it, and the Host instructed them in the planting and cultivating of the garden.

And Adam tilled the garden and was unclothed, but did not know it, and he was not ashamed.

The Lord spoke these words to them.

From every tree of the garden you may eat, but from the tree of learning the knowledge of good and evil you shall not eat, for in the day that you eat thereof you shall surely die (Gen. 2:17 paraphrased).

And after the conclusion of a thousand years, the serpent came and approached the woman. The serpent said to the woman, "Hath not the Lord commanded you, saying, ye shall not eat of every tree of the garden?"

And Eve said to the serpent, "We may eat of the fruit of the trees of the garden, but of the fruit of the tree of learning the knowledge of good and evil which is in the midst of the garden, the Lord said, 'ye shall not eat of it, neither shall ye touch it, lest ye die.'"

The serpent said to the woman, "Ye shall not surely die. For the Lord knows that in whatever day ye should eat of it, your eyes would be opened and ye would be as gods knowing good and evil as do the *beney 'elohim.*"

And the woman saw that the tree was good for food and that it was pleasant to the eyes to look upon and beautiful to contemplate.

Now the serpent was in the Garden of Delight as well as the *beney 'elohim.* These "sons of God" (*beney 'elohim*) had access to the garden and were known to Adam and Eve. Adam and Eve were familiar with these other worldly beings known as gods, and they were spectacular creatures to behold in their goings and comings; the serpent used these spectacular beings to tempt Adam. These beings were at first called "Watchers."

The Watchers were humanoids, composed of a physical and spiritual nature. They are specific angels given charge to watch over humanity. Watchers originally were physical, but they attained ascension and immortally upon their home world sometime in the vast eons past and were given by God the ability to convert themselves to energy for interstellar travel.

The Watchers undertook the task at God's command to observe the inhabitants of the Earth, but this undertaking would eventually lead to the downfall of some of them. Each Watcher possessed vast mental, physical, and energy-manipulating powers. They had the power to manipulate energy even in the electromagnetic spectrum.

The serpent was not a snake as we know it today, although it was cursed to become one.

The serpent was, according to the Hebrew Bible, *aw-room' or* subtle, meaning he had intelligence with a cautious clever character. The serpent in all of his cautiousness was also the most beautiful of beasts and the most exalted of all beasts. The serpent had intelligence with language and often spoke with Adam and Eve.

This familiarity created an environment where caution was thrown to the wind. We have recorded only one of several conversations between Eve and the serpent, but assuredly there were many. Otherwise, common sense would tell you that such a conversation would have alerted Eve to something being badly wrong. Remember, Adam and Eve had shared the garden with the serpent for nearly a thousand years!

And the serpent said unto the woman, "Ye shall not surely die: For the Lord doth know that in the day ye eat thereof, then your eyes shall be opened, and ye shall be as gods, knowing good and evil" (Gen. 3:4-5).

This passage shows there had already been made a distinction between good and evil, although Adam and Eve were blind to it. It is knowledge that Adam and Eve desired–knowledge that had been forbidden. This fruit of the tree of learning the knowledge of good and evil, though often portrayed as an apple, was not an apple.

The etymology of the words *tree* and *fruit* seems to point to a sort of vine resembling a grapevine, and legend has it that its fragrance extended to a considerable distance.

So what was the real temptation? What had Adam seen that he wanted? The temptation of the tree was to acquire a knowledge that Adam had seen. What knowledge could have been seen or could have been displayed by these *beney 'elohim,* and *w*hy was this knowledge forbidden to Adam? What did the Lord not want Adam to experience?

Adam and Eve sought to acquire a forbidden knowledge, something they saw displayed before them, something that could be eaten, something when eaten would "make them wise." When one was "wise," one would be imbued with such wisdom as to change their physical presence; otherwise, why would they have wanted it? Remember, Eve was attracted to the fruit, or rather to what could happen when one ate the fruit.

The fruit of the forbidden tree was most likely a hallucinogen that caused an intense spiritual experience, during which the user would feel contact with a greater spiritual or cosmic order. This experience would be much like what users experience today with hallucinogens.

Being inebriated allowed one to converse with the gods; thus, inebriation and inspiration have often been synonymous from the dawn of civilization.

Just imagine these *beney 'elohim* staggering around "tripping out" while eating the fruit of the forbidden tree. Why they were allowed to do this we are not told, but it was expressly forbidden to Adam and Eve.

Adam and Eve, in eating the forbidden fruit, were trying to access the divine in a backdoor manner. Their goal was to reach the Lord under their own power rather than by the prescribed route, which was waiting until the Lord decided to come and walk in the garden with them in the cool of the day.

Eve, having taken the fruit, offered it to Adam **beside her**. They did eat. The eyes of both were opened with the realization of deception, and they perceived that they were naked with shame. They sewed fig leaves together and made themselves aprons that went around their waists to hide their shame. They soon heard the voice of the Lord walking in the garden in the late afternoon or "cool of the day." Both hid themselves from the face of the Lord in the midst of the trees of the garden.

The Lord called to Adam and said to him, "Adam, where are you?"

Adam answered, "I heard your voice as you walked in the garden, and I feared greatly because I was naked, and I hid myself."

The Lord said to him, "Who told you that you were naked? Have you eaten of the tree concerning which I told thee not to eat?"

Adam said, "The woman whom you gave me, she gave me of the tree, and I did eat."

The Lord said to the woman, "Why have you done this?"

The woman said, "The serpent deceived me, and I ate."

The Lord said to the serpent, "Because thou hast done this, you are cursed above all cattle and above all the brute beasts of the earth, and on your belly you shall crawl, and you shall eat dust all the days of your life. I will put hostility between you and humanity, and between the fallen angels and Eve's descendants. A descendant of Eve will bruise your head–that is, he shall overwhelm you, but you will only bruise his heel."

To the woman the Lord said, "I will greatly multiply thy pains and thy groaning in childbirth, and you must submit to your husband, and your husband shall rule over you."

To Adam the Lord said, "Because you have hearkened to the voice of your wife and eaten of the tree concerning which I commanded you not to eat, cursed is the ground for thy sake. With pain, you shall cultivate the ground all the days of your life. Thorns and thistles will the ground bear. With the sweat of your brow, you will make your bread until the day you return to the earth out of which you were taken. From earth you were taken, and to earth you will return."

The Lord made for Adam and his wife Eve garments of leopard skin and clothed them.

The Lord said, "Behold, Adam is become as one of us to know good and evil, and now lest at any time he stretch forth his hand and take of the Tree of Life and eat and live forever, we must send him out of the Garden of Delight."

So the Lord sent Adam and Eve forth out of the Garden of Delight to cultivate the ground out of which he was taken. On that day the Lord closed the mouth of all beasts so that they could no longer speak, for they had all spoken one with another in the Hebrew tongue while in the Garden of Delight.

He sent out of the Garden of Delight all flesh that was in the Garden of Delight and scattered all flesh according to its kind unto the places that had been created for them.

Adam, passing out of the garden, passed by the tree of learning the knowledge of good and evil and saw the appearance of it had changed and how it had shriveled.

The Lord then barred Adam and Eve from the garden by an ever-turning, fiery, flaming, and sharp sword of the cherub lest they decide to return to the garden and eat of the Tree of Life.

Upon being expelled from the garden, Adam looked back at the gate of the garden, and seeing the cherub with the sword of flashing fire in his hand, feared greatly. Adam and Eve grew faint with fear, and their bodies trembled as their hearts beat ever so loudly in their breasts. They wondered what would become of them.

The Watchers continued to watch over humanity.

After the Lord had driven man out of the garden, there were trials and many burdens put upon the first man and woman.

Adam and Eve walked from the garden as they were commanded, and as they walked, the sky began to dim, and a bright star arose.

They followed the star until they came to a large body of water. As exhaustion took hold, they drifted off to sleep with a rock for a pillow.

Morning came, and as the sun arose and fog dissipated, they could see an island a short distance from the shore. Enchanted with this island, they fashioned a crude raft and floated to the shore of the island. They walked the ground, not knowing where they were. They came upon a cave, and there they took shelter. Until this day it is called the Cave of Regrets.

The Lord said to Adam, "I have set six days that you and your descendants shall be vagabonds upon the earth; on the sixth day I shall send the Jesus that created you and against whom you have sinned, and He shall redeem you and your descendants. The Dark Lords of this world shall put Him to death, but upon the third day He shall arise."

When Adam heard these words from the Lord, he did not understand the meaning of them. His thoughts were that there would be only six days for him until his death. He cried and pleaded with the Lord.

Then the Lord had mercy upon him and explained to him that these days were thousands of years and how at the end of time Jesus would come and save him and his descendants.

Adam and Eve's abode was the Cave of Regrets. However, they were often overcome with sadness at having been barred from the Garden of Delight.

In addition, when Adam looked at his flesh, it was no longer of a bright nature covered in fire and light. He also was no longer able to see angels ascending and descending from heaven.

His eyes, which had once beheld them, could no longer see. He cried discordantly and bemoaned what he had done.

In his remorse, he said to Eve, "Look at this cave that is to be our home! It is gloomy, small, and narrow with floors of rocks and sand! How we have fallen! What is this cave compared to the Garden of Delight with its spaciousness, brightness, and its wonderful fruit trees?"

Adam and Eve stood and prayed in the cave, speaking Hebrew, the first language and the language that the Lord shall reestablish upon the Earth at the end of time.

Eve said, "O Lord, you caused Adam to slumber, and you took a rib from his side to make me in his image, a likeness of brightness and forbiddingness, and covered me in fire." Eve cried bitterly with great sorrow.

The Lord said to them, "In the garden you transgressed of your own free will. You transgressed through your desire for an altered state. You ate of the tree of learning the knowledge of good and evil, which I commanded you not.

"Therefore, I denied you the brightness in which you were then immersed, a bright fire from your loins downward and from your loins upward.

"I created the Dark Prince Lucifer, and he sought Godhood for himself. For this transgression, I hurled him down from the heavenly realm so that he could no longer remain in his first estate.

"He tempted you through your friend the serpent.

"Thus have you transgressed my mandate, and therefore, I have expelled you from the Garden of Delight and brought all these sorrows upon you."

When Adam and Eve heard these words from the Lord, their hearts grew even fainter.

However, the Lord had pity on them and said, "O Adam, I will let you return to the garden when my covenant with you, at the end of time, is satisfied. I have sworn by Myself when the covenant is satisfied, then I will return you to the garden and your descendants."

Adam continued to mourn over his plight on the island.

Then he said to the Lord, "O Lord, take my soul, and let these burdens be passed from me." But the Lord said to Adam, "[3] Be encouraged; I will come down from heaven and shall take upon

---

[3]   It could hardly escape our notice that man's understanding of God does not go well with his belief that God once assumed finite, human form in Christ Jesus. Theologians refer to this as the "Absolute Paradox," the presence of God in time. How could God enter time without ceasing to be the eternal? How could the creator become the creature and subject Himself to time? Fortunately He tells us how: *Christ Jesus, who subsisting in the form of God, thought it not robbery to be equal with God, but emptied* [κενόω] *Himself, taking the form of a slave, having become in the likeness of men and being found in fashion as a man* (Phil 2:6). The KJV version of the Bible says that he made himself of no reputation [κενόω]. The word used here is *ken-o'-o,* and it means *to empty.* Christ Jesus emptied Himself of the prerogatives of Divinity; in human form He was unable to be everywhere at once and subjected Himself to what we call the Absolute Paradox!

myself the flesh of your descendants. I will take on myself the infirmities of death from which you will suffer."

Although they did not understand, they were encouraged.

The next day, the serpent saw Adam and Eve.

It plotted to kill them both. "Because of Adam and Eve, I have to crawl upon my belly."

Then with great veracity, the serpent prepared to attack Adam and Eve, but the Lord intervened.

Adam continued to complain before the Lord of the harsh burdens put upon him. In His mercy, the Lord spoke to encourage Adam. He said, "At the end of time when you shall see perplexity of nations and the moon as blood, I shall bring your descendants out from among the nations and into the garden. I shall uphold My promise and having none greater, I have sworn."

Upon hearing this, they didn't fully understand but strengthened themselves nevertheless.

Then the lovely couple took rocks and built an altar. Upon the altar they offered a lamb unto the Lord. They were instructed to pour water from a spring which flowed of its own accord upon the offering. The Lord accepted their offering! Fire fell from heaven and consumed the offering and hungrily licked the water from the stones.

This was the first sacrifice Adam made to the Lord, and so it became his custom and pattern to do so.

Adam and Eve's dark home resembled more a prison than a safe haven of comfort. Adam continued to bemoan his plight and to cry before the Lord. God heard their cries.

"Adam, let your soul be peaceful until the accomplishment of all time. Then I shall show your descendants compassion and bring them into delightfulness, where there is neither pain, nor sorrow, nor suffering. I will bring them to a place of permanent joy in which the light never fails. I shall bring your descendants to a Garden of Delight that shall never pass away and to a Tree of Life which shall never be taken away."

Then He showed Adam the clear and pure river of the Tree of Life, bright as crystal, pure to the taste, and unlike anything else; no longer proceeding from the depths of the earth, but proceeding forth out of the throne of the Lord.

This Tree of Life produced twelve fruits, and its leaves were for the healing of Adam's descendants. He showed Adam night would be no longer, nor a need for lamps, or even the light of the sun; the Lord would be the Light.

The Lord explained to Adam why first there had to be a time of distress. Many of Adam's offspring would sleep in the dust of the earth until awakened, some to eternal life in the Garden of Delight, while others would know shame and eternal derision in the Lake of Fire. Adam's children who trusted in the Lord and His Christ will shine as the brightest of the stars of heaven.

The Lord continued, "Adam, in a time of distress, your descendants shall blow the trumpet in Zion and sound an alarm on my holy mountain, and every person of the Earth shall know to shake and tremble for the Day of the Lord will be at hand. It will be a day of gloom, a day of clouds, and a day of thick darkness. As a fog spreads over the mountains, there will be placed over Israel a great number of people who are strong.

"A fire will go before these people and behind them, making the land desolate by burning. Nothing shall escape it because of the great heat. Israel's enemies shall come in battle array with all sorts of instruments of war and make a great noise; they shall be mighty and set themselves in battle array. When these invaders fall upon the sword, they shall not be wounded, for they shall be invincible. Israel shall be much afraid before these invaders.

"The heavens shall quake before them, and the sun and moon shall turn dark, and the stars shall remove their unblemished shining. Nevertheless, take heart before this comes to pass. I will pour out my spirit upon all your descendants. Your sons and your daughters shall prophesy, your old men shall dream dreams, and your young men shall see visions.

"Know of a surety, I will pour out my spirit upon my servants in those days, and I shall fill the heavens above and the earth beneath with blood, fire, and pillars of smoke. The sun shall be turned into darkness and the moon into blood before this great and terrible Day of the Lord. It shall come to pass, that whosoever calls my name will be delivered.

"I say unto the descendants of Adam, pull together and come, all ye who trust not in the Lord, come and assemble yourselves together in the valley of Jehoshaphat, for there I will sit to judge you and the nations round about. A multitude will come into the valley of decision, for the day of the Lord is near. I shall roar out of my holy hill Zion and utter My voice from the Temple Mount, and the heavens and the earth shall shake! The Lord will be the hope of His people and the strength of the children of Israel."

The Lord spoke again to Adam. "Complain no more, for thou shalt rest and stand in thy lot at the end of days."

Then when Adam heard these words from the Lord, he and Eve worshiped before Him, and their hearts were comforted.

When Lucifer saw how the Lord had accepted their offering, he ported from the spiritual realm and appeared as a phantom to Adam. He began by transforming the fallen angels into specters of flashing fire and light in order to deceive Adam.

He then placed a throne near the entrance to the cave with twenty-four small thrones around about it.

It illuminated the cave, filling it with brightness. He then led the fallen angels to chant and cast their crowns from their heads to the ground before him, honoring him, the Dark Prince.

The Dark Prince hoped hereby to again deceive Adam with this display of worship and adoration, confident that Adam would think that it was the Host sent from the Lord and that Lucifer's dark angels were the exalted angels of light. He fooled himself into believing that Adam might, upon seeing them, bow and worship.

Thereby Lucifer might deceive Adam and Eve, hoping it might once again bring about Adam's demise.

Eve saw this display and, thinking it was real, said to Adam, "Look at this great host of angels singing and worshiping!" So the deception was working.

As soon as Adam began to pray–for he knew Eve had been deceived before–the Lord sent the captain of the Host, and he appeared to Adam and Eve at the entrance to the cave. The captain of the Host said to Adam, "O Adam, fear not, for I am sent from the Lord to you. The display you have seen was intended to further deceive you."

Then the captain of the host challenged Lucifer, saying, "May the Lord remove your deception!"

Instantly, Lucifer changed from masquerading as an angel of light to the hideous monster he truly was.

The captain of the Host said, "This hideous form is for your sake, Adam, that you might see him as he is." Then the Lord drove away the Prince and his fallen angels. The captain of the Host said, "Fear not; the Lord who inhabits eternity will strengthen you."

The fallen angels disappeared, and the captain of the Host ascended back into the heavenly realm, leaving Adam and Eve alone once more.

As the dim light of morning pierced the opening of their dwelling, a thought entered into Adam and Eve's hearts to return to the garden from whence they had been cast out.

When Lucifer, who hovered close by, saw what direction they were headed, he gathered his lords. They flew upon a cloud, surrounding Adam and Eve with the purpose of deceiving them. Then the Dark Prince, the abhorrence of all good, said to Adam, "O Adam, I am an angel of the great Lord.

"He has sent me to bring you to the garden and to raise you to your former self, returning you again to the Garden of Delight." These words delighted the hearts of Adam and Eve.

There was one mightier than the deceiver who inhabited eternity and who watched to see who they would obey.

As Adam and Eve drew close to the mountain, a very high mountain which was near the approach to the garden, the Dark Lord enticed them and encouraged them to climb to the top. Secretly, he desired to throw them down and kill them, thus eliminating them from the face of the Earth. He wanted supreme control so that the Earth might remain to him and his fallen angels alone.

However, when the captain of the Host saw that the fallen angels wished to throw Adam to the ground, he forbad the fallen angels to harm Adam. The enemy and his hosts fled in fear.

But Adam and Eve remained on the top of the mountain, and from there they could see the garden. Adam cried out to the Lord and begged and prayed for forgiveness. He was heard. God considered the mediation of Adam's heart and forgave him.

The Lord commanded the host to bear up Adam and Eve, bring them down from the top of the high mountain, and take them to their dwelling.

After these things, God spoke to Adam.

Herein is a parable, who has believed my account, and to whom is the arm of the Lord revealed?

My servant was taken from prison and from judgment, and cut off out of the land of the living, and for the transgression of the seed of Adam he was stricken. Yet it pleases the Lord to bruise him; he will put him to grief, and when his soul has become an offering for sin, the Lord shall see of the travail of his soul, and shall be satisfied (Isaiah 53, paraphrased).

When Adam had heard this parable, he gave praise to the Lord. He and Eve worshiped and gave thanks that the Lord had dealt mercifully with them.

A POEM

The Creator became the creature
To destiny bear the law's demand,
For sin to atone, that God might be alone,
Only Him having atoned. Suffer He must,
Sin and anguish burdened,
Hell's destiny for so much.
Judgment must prevail in hell's fiery grasp!
God's soul must atone for judgment past.

My sin must prevail, to judgment obtain.
The soul of God travail He did,
And answered law's demand.
Cursed was He at God's command.
Lightened are we at justice's demand.
Sins no longer to bear,
And mourned by He who must dare.
So suffered He did. Upward He arose.
Judgment satisfied. Love shown
And sin atoned! The soul of God destined
Up from hell's fiery grasp at last.

CK Quartermn

THE DARK LORDS

In the days of Jared, the fallen angels descended from the heavenly realm and took wives unto themselves of the daughters of Adam; this was an abomination in the sight of the Lord.

It was the first time the fallen angels did this, but it was not the last. These beings of the realm were never intended to procreate with humanity; in fact, they were expressly forbidden to do so. These Dark Lords, beings who kept not their own "domain," are those referred to in the Hebrew writings as those who sinned during the days of Noah.

And the angels which kept not their first estate, but left their own habitation (Jude 1:6).

THESE *FALLEN ANGELS* [37] ARE called by many names. Sometimes they are known as the Grigori, Gibborim, and Watchers.

They appear in the mythology and folklore of many diverse cultures, sometimes described as beings that came from the stars and even calling themselves star gods.

The emperors of Japan and the kings of the Aztecs and Mayans are said to be descendants of the star gods, or fallen angels. Every culture has legends of so-called visitors from the stars; in reality, I believe they were the Dark Lords. In the Book of Jubilees, the Book of Enoch, and the Book of [38]Daniel, they are known as Watchers.

These stories have their roots in truth. They may be primitive truths, but in one form or fashion, they are based upon fact, and they exist in every culture. An example of one such fable is the myth of the Titans, which were a race of powerful deities in Greek folklore, wherein the younger Olympians overthrew the elder gods. In this saga, the fallen angels are the descendants of Uranus (ruler of the cosmos), who ruled during the legendary "Golden Age."

In this golden age of Greek mythology, Cronus (Ancient Greek Krónos) overthrew Uranus during a ten-year series of battles known as the Battle of the Titans.

These fallen angels have ventured into our dimension several times. The first incursion began before the Great Flood when some two hundred fallen angels followed the Dark Lord called Samyaza and elected him their leader.

The full number of fallen angels is unknown; however, a small number under Samyaza swore an oath together to materialize into this realm and to perform the deed of cohabiting with the daughters of men. They forsook their own realm in direct opposition to the command of the Lord.

When the fallen angels saw the daughters born to the children of men, they became entranced with them, saying one to one another, "Come, we must take to ourselves concubines from the descendants of men."

These fallen angels under Samyaza conspired together to take upon themselves bodies of flesh in order to marry the daughters of men.

Early man painted what he saw: half-human/ half-animal creatures: the hybrids and the nephilim!

This they knew would be a one-way trip, knowing they would be barred from returning back into the spiritual realm having once disobeyed the Lord's command. But, nevertheless, they harkened to their chosen leader, Samyaza.

Samyaza said to them, "I fear that you may not fulfill this venture, and I alone shall suffer for so terrible a crime."

They answered and said to him, "We all pledge and bind ourselves by fears that we will not change our mind and hearts, but we will fulfill this venture."

The two hundred swore together, and all bound themselves by the fears. The whole number, with their leaders, descended upon [39]Mount Hermon in the days of Jared. All of the Watchers who materialized into this realm took wives, cohabiting with them and teaching them all manner of wickedness, sorcery, and witchcraft.

Wickedness continued to increase, and fornication by the fallen angels rampaged throughout the Earth. The fallen angels continued to transgress the commandment until they had corrupted all of mankind.

The nephilim were the children who resulted from these unions, and they were called the heroes of old, men of renown. They became the heroes of Greek and Roman mythology. The children of the nephilim gave birth to the elioud.

The nephilim and the elioud were quite likely the builders of the large objects found around the world, objects like the pyramids, Stonehenge, and ancient temples.

This is the kind of race that provides plausible and understandable explanations of the many megaliths and early structures, such as the ancient obelisk and the stone statues called moai on Easter Island.

Early man painted what he saw: half-human/half-animal creatures: the hybrids and the nephilim! Examples of such creatures include Khnum, the Egyptian ram-headed nephilim; the chimera, a creature with the body and head of a lioness, a tail that ended in a snake's head, and a third head—that of a goat—that arose on its back at the center of its spine; the winged sphinx, such as the one portrayed on the wall of the palace of Darius the Great during the Persian Empire at Susa (480 BC); Centaurus, a half-horse/half-human creature that is said to have drawn the chariot of Constantine the Great; Bastet, an Egyptian half- cat/half-human nephilim; the minotaur, a creature with the head of a bull on the body of a man; Anubis, a jackal-headed nephilim of Egyptian culture; and Thoth, a nephilim of Egyptian culture with the head of a bird.

A casual perusal of mythology and folklore will render hundreds of creatures. Some of the better known are from the continent of India and are depicted with either four heads and four arms or having three eyes. However, there is none more colorful than Vishnu, a major Hindu god who assumes various manifestations and even rides on a snake. However, most are generally depicted in humanoid or partially humanoid form. Some are grotesque, having an elephant head or the head of a monkey. Hinduism even has a mythology of giants who are said to be of monstrous size and have a great hunger.

Lesser-known giants are those from the South Sea Islands or the Baltic, whereas the British giants are much better known. Even the Irish have a race of giants inhabiting the island in ancient times. They were said to have had the body of a man and the head of a goat.

America has of course had its Paul Bunyan, but much lesser known are giants such as the Goatman and a similar creature, Kentucky's Pope Lick Monster.

Described as a hybrid half human and half goat, the Goatman is horned, hoofed, and appears to be a modern day satyr. Eye-witnesses claim that this Goatman is not a mythological being but a real creature. The first report of this creature was in 1957, when witnesses reported seeing a hairy, horned monster. Following that, in 1962 the Goatman is said to have killed no less than fourteen people. Eyewitnesses claimed that the Goatman violently hacked its victims to pieces with an axe, all the while emitting grisly sounds.

Early man painted what he saw, half-human/half-animal nephilim! As I stated earlier, I have seen one with my own eyes and will share that encounter in more detail later on in this book.

The Babylonians, Greeks, Romans, and all ancient cultures recorded a race of beings displaying great powers of intellect, huge size, and great strength. These nearly universal records give testimony of very large beings, generally from eight to twelve feet tall, but some as tall as thirty-six feet. Some weighed over a thousand pounds.

According to Julius Caesar, the Gauls asserted that they were descended from gods (fallen angels), and he linked them to the Druids.

This establishes that the Gaul peoples are the same people as the modern Celts.

Let's look at what men from ancient times have said about these beings. We'll start with Julius Caesar.

In 56 BC, Julius Caesar wrote, "The nation of all the Gauls are extremely devoted to superstitious rites; and on that account they who are troubled with unusually severe diseases, and they who are engaged in battles and dangers, either sacrifice men as victims, or vow that they will sacrifice them, and employ the Druids as the performers of those sacrifices; because they think that unless the life of a man be offered for the life of a man, the mind of the immortal gods cannot be rendered propitious, and they have sacrifices of that kind ordained for national purposes. Others have figures of vast size, the limbs of which were formed of [strong flexible twigs] they fill with living men, which being set on fire, the men perish enveloped in the flames. They consider that the oblation of such as have been taken in theft, or in robbery, or any other offense, is more acceptable to the immortal gods.

"But when a supply of that class is wanting, they have recourse to the oblation of even the innocent.

"All the Gauls assert that they are descended from the god Dis, and say that this tradition has been handed down by the Druids." (Caesar's Commentaries on the Gallic War, chapter 16)

In 2BC, Polybius wrote, "The Romans were terrified by the fine order of the Celtic host, and the dreadful din, for there were innumerable horn -blowers and trumpeters, and... the whole army were shouting their war-cries....Very terrifying too were the appearance and the gestures of the naked warriors in front, all in the prime of life and finely built men, and all in the leading companies richly adorned with gold torcs and armlets."

Diodorus Siculus, 25 BC, wrote, "Physically the Celts are terrifying in appearance, with deep sounding and very harsh voices.

They are tall in stature, with rippling muscles under clear white skin, they look like wood demons. They wore golden necklaces."

Virgil, 1 BC, wrote, "Golden is their hair and golden their garb. They are resplendent in their striped cloaks, and their milk-white necks are circled with gold."

> ## Noah was a righteous man; his genetic record was uncorrupted by nephilim DNA.

This quote by Virgil leads one author to link the gold necklaces worn by the Celtic people to the biblical accounts of the Anakim which were one of the tribes listed as giants in the Bible. The author says the word *Anaq* in some contexts means "a necklace so tight as to appear to be strangling," and that the use of this word suggests that the most noticeable feature of the descendants of Anak was a tight chain about the neck. This leads to the supposition that the giant Anakim pushed out of Canaan by the Israelites eventually settled what are now the Celtic nations.

The Sumatrans had Gilgamesh, the Babylonian king who is pictured on stone tablets recovered from Mesopotamia. He is depicted holding two lions by the leg, one in each hand. It is said he was able to take out a lion single-handedly because of his size and incredible strength.

If these representations on these stone tables are to scale, then Gilgamesh would have weighed over one thousand pounds.

Gilgamesh is also by legend the offspring of a god.

When the fallen angels of Rahab began to marry the daughters of men, and their children had corrupted the genetic line of men, the Lord said,

I will not work on man's side forever, for he is physical. His genetic line cannot recover from this incursion (Gen. 6:3, paraphrased).

In the six hundredth year of Noah's life, in the second month, the seventeenth day of the month, the same day were all the fountains of the great deep broken up, and the windows of heaven were opened. And the rain was upon the earth forty days and forty nights (Gen. 7:11-12).

This genetic invasion had to be stopped! So God gave the Earth 43,800 days before destruction. This is called the deluge. The Lord sought out and found one man who was perfect in all his generations, one man who was not genetically altered by this incursion. His name was Noe, or Noah.

Before the Flood, the giants, the nephilim, the children of the fallen angels destroyed themselves.

Noah was a righteous man; his genetic record was uncorrupted by nephilim DNA.

*These are the generations of Noah: Noah was a just man and **perfect** in his generations, and Noah walked with God* (Gen. 6:9) (KJV).

The Hebrew word for perfect is tamıym (pronounced tawmeem) which means "without blemish, undefiled, sound, and whole." It is the same word used in "*Your lamb shall be without blemish*" (Exodus 12:5), referring to the lamb that was used in temple worship.

Why would God be concerned with the lamb's distinct physical characteristics or Noah's physical appearance? Because physical characteristics can show underlying genetic defects in lambs and people. There are specific defects on a genetic level that are specific to the offspring of fallen angels. These hybrids have the distinct physical characteristic of six fingers and six toes. This defect is explicit to the offspring of the fallen ones.

Noah was a righteous man, but also perfect in all of his generations. Nephilim DNA did not corrupt his DNA, and therefore he alone could replenish the earth.

Later, when the Law was given to the Israelites, certain non-Jewish races could not convert to Judaism and enter the Temple unto the tenth generation. This was to ensure that no one with nephilim DNA would enter the Temple.

Before the Flood, the giants, the nephilim, the children of the fallen angels destroyed themselves.

[40]*And He sent His sword into their midst that each should slay his neighbour, and they began to slay each other till they all fell by the sword and were destroyed from the earth* (Jubilees 5:5-9).

It is recorded by another in the Book of Enoch;

[41]*Let them perish by mutual slaughter; for length of days shall not be theirs.* (Enoch 10:6)

That the offspring of the fallen angels were destroyed by turning against one another is affirmed by both the Book of Enoch and the Book of Jubilees.

This would explain why they left Noah alone while he built the ark; otherwise, Noah would not have been allowed by these giants to finish it.

The Great Flood destroyed man and beast. This is attested to in the Books of Enoch and Jubilees as well as Genesis.

It is said that the Book of Enoch was left out of the Bible because of its claim that fallen angels fornicated with man and beast.

We don't want to admit that such things could happen; then we don't have to face it; we don't have to see the ugly truth. The Dark Lords have worked for thousands of years to remove the supernatural elements from the Bible.

Then came the flood upon the earth, namely, owing to the fornication wherein the Watchers against the law of their ordinances went a whoring after the daughters of men, and took themselves wives of all which they chose: and they made the beginning of uncleanness. And they begat sons, the nephilim, *and they were all unlike, and they devoured one another: and the Giants slew one man another* (Book of Jubilees).

This wickedness of the fallen angels brought about the Flood; their children turned upon one another and killed one another. The Lord brought the Great Flood to destroy the DNA that defiled mankind and the creatures of the Earth.

> **Before the Flood, the giants, the nephilim, the children of the fallen angels destroyed themselves.**

The terms used to describe the nephilim offspring indicate the nature of the sin of the fallen angels involved. The term *nephilim* means giant and is derived from the primitive root *naphal*, meaning to fall down, cast down, and fall away. *Raphah* is the root word used for ghosts of the dead, shades, and spirits.

According to Enoch, the two hundred fallen angels who had intermarried with the daughters of men in the days of Jarad were chained under hell in darkness.

The desert which is in Dudael (Judean Desert) was opened, and the offenders were thrust down into Tartarus and covered with sharp stones and chains of darkness to await the Day of Judgment. (Tartarus is the deepest abyss of Hades, and is the same as the underworld, or abode of the dead.) But what of their final resting place at the end of days?

[42] Enoch says, *He took me to a place in which there was darkness and blackness. And there, I saw only an uninhabited barren spot, and horrible.*

I saw the evil ones bound together, like an enormous mountain, and it had burning flickering flames encircling and enfolding. I looked.

This great blazing, blistering fire gleamed in a dazzling way, and in the middle there was a void. Flames flickered around empty space, and profound was its bottomlessness.

Its sheer size was too great to envision. I was unable to determine its beginning or end.

What is this place? It is a black hole, and it will be the fallen angels' final resting place, the pit of fire as mentioned in the book of Revelation.

In the first incursion before the Great Flood, under their leader Samyaza, the fallen angels cohabited with all that they pleased. Again, after the Great Flood, some of the evil angels transgressed the commandment and married women. When the children of Israel, a thousand years later, attempted to enter the Promised Land, they found these offspring, the children of the Dark Lords, the nephilim, blocking their entrance.

And they brought up an evil report of the land which they had searched unto the children of Israel, saying, "The land, through which we have gone to search it, is a land that eateth up the inhabitants thereof; and all the people that we saw in it are men of a great stature. And there we saw the giants, the sons of Anak, which come of the giants: and we were in our own sight as grasshoppers, and so we were in their sight" (Num. 13:32-33) (KJV).

These giants meeting the Israelites were alluded to in Genesis 6:4. *There were giants in the earth in those days; and **also after that.***

This verse suggests that further incursions will take place and explains why the Lord commanded the total extermination of the Canaanites. Remember, He had earlier in history annihilated the human race with the Flood.

Many have argued the reality of the incursion of these fallen angels into our realm, but the evidence is overwhelming. In one of humanity's oldest writings, the Hebrew Old Testament, the fallen angels are called the *beney 'elohim.*

*And it came to pass, when men began to multiply on the face of the
earth, and daughters were born unto them, That the sons of God (beney
'elohim) saw the daughters of men that they were fair; and they took them
wives of all which they chose. And the LORD said, My spirit shall not
always strive with man, for that he also is flesh: yet his days shall be an
hundred and twenty years. There were* [43]*giants in the earth in those days;
and also after that, when the sons of God came in unto the daughters of
men, and they bare children to them, the same became mighty men which
were of old, men of renown* (Gen. 6:1-9).

There are three possible understandings for the usage of the term
"sons of God" or *beney 'elohim* as found in the ancient Hebrew
Scriptures, but we shall see that only one understanding fits the
text of the Hebrew Bible.

The sons of God or *beney 'elohim* are thought by some to be
only the sons of Seth, and the daughters of men the descendants
of Cain. In this view, the crime was the marriage of the holy line
of Seth to the unholy line of Cain.

The "sons of Seth" interpretation appeared about 400 AD and
was the first dispute to the angel view that a majority of both Jews
and Christians had held prior to that time. Some famous scholars
still teach this unscriptural view.

There are serious problems with this theory. First of all, the
phrase "the line of Seth" is nowhere defined in the Hebrew Bible
as a holy line of people. Also, the theory fails to take into account
that nowhere in history is it evidenced that intermarriage of any
people or culture produces a giant, nor did the Lord destroy or
threaten to destroy a race or culture because of intermarriages. In
spite of modern day proponents of this theory, this argument is
not convincing. It is pure eisegesis: reading into the text what is
obviously not there in order to prove one's own ideas.

The early church fathers, Justin Martyr, Irenaeus, Athenagoras, Tertullian, Lactantius, Eusebius, and Ambrose all accepted the angel view.

They said, "The angels transgressed and were captivated by love of women and begat children who are called giants." This is recorded in vol. 8, pages 85 and 273 of *The Ante-Nicene Fathers.* Only after the fifth century do we find any interpretation other than angels for the *sons of God* or *beney 'elohim.*

The sons of God or *beney 'elohim* are thought by some to be merely rulers, and the daughters of men only the masses; the transgression in this view is polygamy. The evidence for this view is that rulers are often referred to as gods or the offspring of gods. This is an even weaker interpretation.

The problem with this theory is that royalty has not in any way now or in ancient times, or anywhere in the Hebrew Bible, been associated with deity.

The sons of God or *beney 'elohim* are the fallen angels, fallen beings of the heavenly realm, and the "daughters of men" are earthly women. The transgression is marriage and the begetting of children by the fallen angels.

> **The angels transgressed and were captivated by love of women and begat children who are called giants.**

The evidence for this view is given in the New Testament by Jude. According to Jude, these fallen angels, "in like manner [gave] themselves over to fornication, and [went] after strange flesh."

These other-worldly beings could take upon themselves flesh. Abraham's conversation with angels (on their way to destroy Sodom) who appeared to him as humans and even ate the food Abraham prepared for them is proof of that.

Finally, it's also the most natural reading of the verse in light of the offspring being giants.

For some people, saying that the "sons of God" are fallen angels who fornicated with humans poses some contradictions in light of Matthew 22:30. However, when we look at the verse more deeply, it isn't contradictory. Why?

Jesus does not illuminate the sexual activities of angels in Matthew 22:30.

For in the resurrection they (people) neither marry, nor are given in marriage, but are as the angels of God in heaven (Matthew 22:30).

For when they shall rise from the dead, they neither marry, nor are given in marriage; but are as the angels which are in heaven (Mark 12:25).

And Jesus answering said unto them, "The children of this world marry, and are given in marriage: But they which shall be accounted worthy to obtain that world, and the resurrection from the dead, neither marry, nor are given in marriage: Neither can they die any more: for they are equal unto the angels; and are the children of God, being the children of the resurrection" (Luke 20:34-36).

It should be noted that while Jesus states (in Matthew 22:30, Mark 12:25, and Luke 20:34-36) that we will be like the angels, He doesn't say that we or angels are *incapable* of marriage or that angels have never participated in marriage. It also must be noted that the New Testament is talking about the honorable angels, not wicked beings; the point that Jesus makes is that the institution of marriage in heaven isn't necessary.

The institution of marriage will be done away with because of what is stated in Matthew 22:30, Mark 12:25, and Luke 20:34–36 above.

One possible explanation might be an assumption that the human race was initially designed to sexually reproduce within the confines of marriage until the resurrection, but once resurrected, the human race becomes a higher species, a group in which reproduction no longer serves a purpose. We will still have our sexual organs, but these organs will only serve as reminders of our former state.

In the Book of Jubilees, the fallen angels or *beney 'elohim* are called Watchers. It is clear from this text that they were not human but beings of a heavenly realm destined to watch over mankind. However, they transgressed the commandment as we saw in Jude.

The *beney 'elohim* not only co-habited with mankind but also mixed their DNA with animals, producing unnatural beasts such as the pegasus, minotaur, and the unicorn.

This incursion of the fallen angels into our realm is certainly an apostasy and an abomination, the outright breaking of the very laws of nature itself.

The famous Jewish historian Flavius Josephus wrote about this time.

For many angels of God accompanied with women, and begat sons that proved unjust, and despisers of all that was good, on account of the confidence they had in their own strength; for the tradition is, that these men did what resembled the acts of those whom the Grecians call "giants."

The early church distorted the teaching of Genesis 6 by saying that the term "sons of God" in the first verse referred to the God-fearing line of Seth. Certainly, someone might ask how angels from heaven could possibly engage in sexual relations with women from Earth. Some think that a spiritual being must stay a spiritual being.

Abraham entertained angels who became human enough to eat, see, smell, feel, and touch.

And the LORD appeared unto him in the plains of Mamre: and he sat in the tent door in the heat of the day; And he lift up his eyes and looked, and, lo, three men stood by him… under the tree, and they did eat (Gen. 18:1-22) (KJV).

These angels were in human form. They were able to behave in a human manner. It's really not farfetched to believe that they also had the ability to have sexual relations. Many other sources testify that they can have sexual relations and did in Genesis 6. These are some of the ancient sources echoing the same thought:

The Testaments of the Twelve Patriarchs

The Testament of Naphtali, the Eighth Son of Jacob and Bilhah

That ye become not as Sodom, which changed the order of nature. In like manner the Watchers also changed the order of their nature, whom the Lord cursed at the flood, on whose account He made the earth without inhabitants and fruitless (Naphtali 1:26-27).

The Testament of Reuben, the First-Born Son of Jacob and Leah

For thus they (women) allured the Watchers who were before the flood; for as these continually beheld them, they lusted after them, and they conceived the act in their mind; for they changed themselves into the shape of men, and appeared to them when they were with their husbands (Reuben 2:18).

The Book of Jubilees

He called his name Jared, for in his days the angels of the Lord descended on the earth, those who are named the Watchers, that they should instruct the children of men, and that they should do judgment and uprightness on the earth (Jubilees 4:13).

And he (Enoch) testified to the Watchers, who had sinned with the daughters of men; for these had begun to unite themselves, so as to be

defiled, with the daughters of men, and Enoch testified against (them) all (Jubilees 4:22).

And it came to pass when the children of men began to multiply on the face of the earth and daughters were born unto them, that the angels of God saw them on a certain year of this jubilee, that they were beautiful to look upon; and they took themselves wives of all whom they chose, and they bare unto them sons, and they were giants (Jubilees 4:1-2).

Owing to the fornication wherein the Watchers against the law of their ordinances went a whoring after the daughters of men, and took themselves wives of all which they chose (Jubilees 7:21).

EZEL

Ezel watches a young girl as she goes about life.

YOU MIGHT ASK HOW COULD an angel called a Watcher, given the responsibility of watching over humanity, fall into the sin of fornication. That they did is clear, but the reasoning might seem foreign, so I have decided to add a window into the life of a Watcher. This is the only fictional character in this book, and we will use him to look into the thinking of the Watchers and the struggle which perhaps raged in their minds before cohabitating with the daughters of men. We will call him Ezel.

He watches her bathe in the stream. Her beauty spellbinds him. Her hair is dark, and curls naturally flow down over her shoulders to the middle of her back. She bathes herself in the fresh spring water.

It is cool, tumbling down from the mountains, and makes her skin tingle. The spring is an old one upon her father's land bequeathed by her grandfather Jared. The angel thinks her skin resembles spun silk, and she is the fairest of all women. Her cheeks are beautiful, and her eyes are likened to doves.

The smell of her ointments is better than all spices. They have drawn him, and he will run after her. He has watched her many days from her youth when she tended her father's flock.

She lies down to sleep and muses at the cedar rafters and beams of the ceilings. He longs to hold her and kiss her. His unrequited love burns within him. However, he remembers the commandment. He cannot come into this realm and reveal his love for her.

The angel watches her behind the wall, looking through the windows, peeping through the lattices. Though she knows it not, she is never alone. He is unseen, lurking in the bright of day and in the dark of night; he is always there.

Winter passes. Flowers bloom in the land. The fig tree puts forth its young figs, and the vines the tender grape.

A scent is in the air.

Ezel thinks to himself, *Arise my love, my fair one, and come away with me.*

But he dares not break the commandment for the Lord had clearly commanded, "Thou shalt not cross the realm and take human form, nor be found in the likeness of flesh."

Azamysa, who sometimes was called Bale, knew the ancient stories. Ezel made a note unto himself to seek him out.

Amber, the sweet young girl, was growing into a beautiful woman. Ezel was becoming bolder—at times, projecting his thoughts into her mind. He hadn't yet broken the commandment, and she wasn't aware of his presence.

Amber was like many of the young girls and women whom the *beney 'elohim* began to watch and to set their affection upon. These Watchers did not start as malevolent spirits but as spirits tasked with the oversight of humans. They had been authorized to help humans in distress and to report to the Lord as to the goings on upon the earth.

The *beney 'elohim* at first did well and obeyed the commandment, but lust began to grow within them.

They began to reveal themselves in small ways. Then as their lust grew within them, they began to act upon these feelings. Finally, breaking the commandment and taking on human flesh, they gave themselves over to fornication and were damned forever.

GOLIATH

There came a day when the Philistines gathered their armies for battle against Israel.

BY RECORD OF HIS SHEER size, Goliath was undoubtedly a nephilim.

Israel under King Saul gathered together in the valley of Elah. Israel, at this time, kept no standing army. King Saul set his army in battle formation to meet the Philistines with the opposing sides facing each other, the Philistines on one mountain peak and Israel on the other with the valley between them. Israel watched as the enemy sent out their champion. His name was Goliath, and he was from a part of Philistia called Gath; **his height was nineteen feet**. He wore a bronze helmet and full body armor; **the body armor weighed one hundred and twenty five pounds**. Over this, **he wore a covering of bronze**. He carried a **javelin of bronze** and a wooden spear. The wooden spear had a blade of bronze that weighed **twenty-five pounds**. A shield bearer carried his shield and readied it for battle.

Goliath called out, taunting Israel and saying, "Why do you approach to battle?

"Can you really defeat me? Draw closer now; you do not have a chance! Let us get this over with. Choose your best man and let him come up to fight me. If he is able to kill me, then we shall leave you alone. But if I kill him, then you shall become slaves to Philistia and shall serve us."

Goliath continued to taunt Israel. "Give me a man, and we will fight together!"

By record of his sheer size, Goliath was undoubtedly a nephilim.

All of Israel heard these taunts of Goliath and were greatly afraid, shaking as they listened.

Three of David's brothers were arrayed in battle formation with Israel. They prepared to fight, but David as the youngest returned from the battle formation to feed his father's flock at Bethlehem.

Goliath taunted Israel morning and evening for forty days. While this taunting took place, David's father Jesse said to his youngest son, "Please take to your brothers this roasted grain and these ten loaves of bread, for they are hungry and do not have enough provisions to last.

"Also, David, take cheese to the commander of your brother's brigade, and you shall visit them before you return to let me know how they are doing."

David rose up early in the morning and left the sheep. He went as his father had commanded him. He came to the army and to his brother's brigade. The men were going out in battle formation, shouting and carrying their swords. Israel and the Philistines set up in battle array with rank aligned with rank, row after row they were lined up man to man. David left the food with the quartermaster. He ran out to meet the army. He found his brothers and inquired as to their welfare.

While David was speaking to his brothers, Goliath called out, taunting Israel. Upon seeing him in all his armor, standing nineteen feet tall, all the men of Israel ran from him. The soldiers of Israel said, "Have you seen Goliath? He is nineteen feet tall! The man who kills him, King Saul will bestow on him great riches and give his daughter to him."

David said, "Who is this Philistine dog that he should reproach the armies of the living God?" No one dared to answer!

David's eldest brother Eliab heard what David said and was angry. He said, "With whom have you left the few sheep in the wilderness? I know you have come down only to see the battle."

David said, "What have I done now?"

David's words were told to Saul, and Saul called for David to be brought before him. David said to Saul, "Let no man's heart fail because of Goliath. I will go and fight with this dog."

Saul said to David, "You are not able to fight this Goliath; he is a giant, and you are but a youth. He is a man of war from his childhood."

David answered, "Your servant has been a shepherd taking care of sheep for his father. A bear came, taking a lamb out of the flock. I went out after him, killed him, and took the lamb out of his mouth. A lion attacked me. I took hold of his hair and killed him. This Philistine dog I shall kill just as I killed the beasts!"

Meanwhile, Goliath continued reproaching the armies of the living God.

David said, "Jehovah, who has delivered me out of the paw of the lion and out of the mouth of the bear, He also shall deliver me from the hand of this Philistine dog."

Saul said to David, "Go, and Jehovah be with you." He clothed David with his own armor. Saul placed a bronze helmet on David's head and girded him with his own sword.

David started to go, but he had never before worn armor. And David said to Saul, "I am not able to go wearing this armor, for it is too heavy."

David took off the armor and instead headed out to face the taunting giant with just his staff in his hand and five smooth stones from valley brook for his sling. He put these into his shepherd's bag.

With his sling in his hand, he approached the giant. The behemoth too came forward with his shield bearer in tow. When the Philistine saw David, he disdained him, seeing how young he was. He said to David, "Am I a dog that you have come to me with sticks?" Goliath laughed while cursing David by his gods.

"Come here, and I will kill you and give your flesh to the birds of the heavens and to the beasts of the field."

David answered, "You come to me with sword, spear, and javelin. However, I am coming to you in the name of the Lord of Hosts, the God of the armies of Israel, whom you have reproached. Today Jehovah shall deliver you into my hand.

"I shall kill you and take off your head. I'll give your carcass to the birds of the air and to the beasts of the earth! All the earth shall know that there is a God in Israel, and all this company shall know that Jehovah does not save by sword nor by spear, but that **the battle belongs to Jehovah**, and He has given you into my hand."

When Goliath arose and drew near to meet the young shepherd boy, David hurried and ran toward the ranks to meet the Philistine. Reaching into his pouch, he took a stone and slung it around and around his head. He let the sling go, and the stone flew from the sling and struck Goliath in the forehead. The stone sank deep into his forehead, almost disappearing, and he fell on his face to the ground. The youth had slain the mighty warrior with the sling and the stone, hitting his mark and killing the giant.

There was no sword in David's hand, so with extraordinary strength, he took Goliath's sword, drawing it out of its sheath. Raising the heavy weapon, he cut off Goliath's head as he had promised. When they saw that their champion warrior was dead, the Philistines fled. The army of Israel and the men of Judah rose up and shouted, and they pursued the Philistines to the gates of Ekron. David took the head of Goliath and brought it to Jerusalem.

It is interesting to note that Goliath and the Philistines worshiped a nephilim. Dagon was the principal god of the Philistines. He was the father of Baal, a nephilim half-human/half-fish hybrid whose upper body was that of a man and the lower body that of a fish. This is attested to by the many coins that have been found in various Philistine cities. The Septuagint text of 1 Samuel 5:2–7 says that both the hands and the head of the image of Dagon were broken off when the ark was captured by the Philistines and taken to the temple of Dagon in Ashdod.

The following morning they found the image of Dagon lying prostrate before the ark. They set the image upright, but again on the morning of the following day they found it prostrate before the ark, but this time with head and hands had been cut off. Thereafter, we are told that no one entered Dagon's temple even "unto this day."

The Babylonians also believed that Dagon was a nephilim. They believed that Dagon emerged from the Erythraean Sea and was part man and part fish.

Josephus mentions a place named Dagon above Jericho, and Dagon is mentioned in passages such as Judges 16:23-24, I Samuel 5, and I Chronicles 10:10.

Giants such as Goliath assuredly existed. Of that there is no doubt. However, there are other things, other unidentified objects or creatures that have been witnessed throughout time and in our current age. Might these unidentified objects or beings also be linked to Lucifer and the fallen angels?

As we have already shown, there was an Ancient Egyptian nephilim called Anubis, who was depicted with the body of a man and the head of a jackal. Anubis was a hybrid, but there were others like him in different parts of the world. The Greeks had Lycaon who, according to myth, had displeased the god Zeus and was changed into a wolf. These hybrids were the inspiration for the werewolves of the Middle Ages.

By record of his sheer size, Goliath was undoubtedly a nephilim.

A renewed interest in werewolves has gained considerable momentum since the growth of the Wiccan movement in the late 20th century. Popularity has skyrocketed with books such as the *Twilight* series. I think it shows a dangerous interest in the occult and the supernatural.

Hollywood tells us that werewolves are linked to the occult and can be felled by a silver bullet. This wild idea demonstrates the devil's dark influence over gullible humanity. Werewolves are real, but they are hybrids, half angel and half wolf – nephilim. Being of such a nature, they are endowed with psychic ability and supernatural powers but are able to die like any human or wolf.

UFO'S

Fallen angels were unable to return to their realm after leaving their original habitation and making the switch into ours.

NEITHER IS THERE ANY EVIDENCE that they were destroyed, or imprisoned by the Lord, after their attempt to keep Israel out of Canaan. The two hundred that cohabited with the daughters of Adam during the days of Noah were certainly imprisoned in Tartarus. **However, there is no mention of punishment for the offending fallen angels after the days of Noah. Therefore, we may assume that they are still among us.**

This same incursion into our realm that took place in Canaan also took place in other areas around the world.

Before settlers from the Old World came to the New World (North America) the Cherokee already knew the fallen angels.

Posing (as they always have) as "star gods," fallen angels visited both North and South America.

The remains of seven to eight-foot tall red-haired giants have been found in the Midwest, specifically in Nevada. The Paiutes, a Native-American tribe indigenous to parts of Nevada, Utah, and

Arizona, told early white settlers about their ancestors' battles with a fierce race of red-haired giants.

According to the August 5, 1947, edition of the San Diego Union, the remains of giants were discovered near the Arizona-Nevada-California wasteland. The giants' remains were still clothed in strange garments.

South America has its Aztec and Mayan legends of visitors from the stars, some predicting a return of the "star gods." Less known, however, are North American legends. Here is one of my favorites, the Cherokee legend of visitors from the stars.

CHEROKEE NATION MEETS FALLEN ANGELS
*As told by the Eastern Band of the Cherokee Tribe

One night a hunting party noticed two lights moving along the top of a distant mountain. They watched until the lights disappeared.

The next night the lights appeared again. The hunting party went to investigate in the daylight and was astounded to discover two strange creatures with small turtlish heads protruding from large, round bodies covered with fine, gray fur. As the breeze ruffled their fur, showers of sparks flew out.

The hunting party carried the weird and wonderful creatures quietly back to their encampment. During the day, they were tame balls of gray fur, but at night, they would grow bright and shine.

> **As we approach the doorstep of the end of time, we will see more of the fallen angels at work.**

The gray creatures didn't seem inclined to try to escape when, on the seventh night, they suddenly rose from the ground in balls of fire. The hunting party stared with mouths agape. Higher and higher, the creatures ascended, while the astonished hunting party watched. At last, they were only two bright points of light in the night sky. Then the terrified hunting party knew that they were stars. This story has been handed down through each generation.

UFOs and alien abductions are taboo subjects for most people, though the sightings seem to be happening all over the world. Reports of alien abductions and UFO's are gaining in the media. I believe they have nothing to do with outer space and *everything* to do with fallen angels, the Dark Lords.

The New Testament states that "as in the **days that were before the flood** they were eating and drinking, marrying and giving in marriage, until the day that Noe entered into the ark, so shall also the coming of the Son of man be" (Matt. 24:38-39) (KJV).

The question is, then, what was happening before the Flood? Remember, if we look back at the Old Testament to see who was marrying in those days, we find that the only details given were regarding the marriages of the sons of God to the daughters of men. As we have already discussed and covered, the fallen angels were mating with the daughters of men. This would explain both the UFO and abduction phenomenon.

All over the world, people are experiencing abductions that they cannot explain.

Where are people supposed to turn if they cannot discuss these strange happenings with their pastors? I believe that these recurring events are directly related to the Bible, and I believe the Lord has called me to make myself available to the people who seek answers for all the strange phenomena.

As we approach the doorstep of the end of time, we will see more of the fallen angels at work. However, as long as pastors and leaders refuse to talk about it, as long as they continue to hold on to the theory that the sons of God or *beney 'elohim* are the sons of

Seth and the daughters of men are the descendants of Cain, then the truth will remain hidden. Remember, the phrase "the line of Seth" is nowhere defined in the Hebrew Bible as a holy line of people. The fallen angels have successfully deceived many religious leaders. People will continue to be abducted, and the fallen angels will continue to manipulate humanity.

Let's take a look at Daniel, where we find another piece of the fallen angel puzzle.

And whereas thou sawest iron mixed with miry clay, they shall mingle themselves with the seed of men (Daniel 2:43).

Daniel offers us the blueprint of both UFOs and alien abductions.

The fallen angels have the following in common with UFOs and alien abduction phenomena: Strange beings abduct women of their choosing at a time of their choosing and impregnate them. The great majority of abductees are women, and some kind of hybrid or nephilim is born as a result of each unholy union.

Let no man deceive you by any means: for that day shall not come, except there come a falling away first (2 Thessalonians 2:3-4).

What kind of event would cause a falling away? One which would deceive, if possible, even the elect? I believe so.

If the fallen angels showed up and claimed to be who they truly are, very few of us would turn away from the Lord to follow them. However, if they showed up and pretended to be extraterrestrials, beings from the stars, people might possibly believe this, especially if accompanied by a dog and pony show.

Expect the government to come forth with "full disclosure" soon. The government will admit a connection with aliens, but it will be in fact a connection with the fallen angels of Rahab, the Dark Lords.

Our government is deceived, believing itself in communication with star-traveling aliens. New movies abound on this theme. TV shows and movies, including *The X-Files, Star Trek*, and a score of others, undergird this reasoning.

> **All research into the UFO and the abduction phenomena indicates an evil influence.**

And for this cause the Lord shall send them strong delusion, that they should believe a lie (2 Thess. 2:11).

Where is deception, but where the fallen angels operate? What is this strong delusion?

The fallen angels will once again come to earth as "star gods," but they are no such thing! That is a great delusion.

They are from another realm, *not* another planet. They will have as their ambassador the Antichrist. They are themselves the beast of the Apocalypse. Their unveiling to the world is but a short time away.

Canadian ex-defense minister Paul Hellyer spoke at the International UFO Conference in February 2011 and stated that there had been a cover up of such incidents as the Roswell Crash. He spoke in the affirmative that the US was withholding contact with aliens. He also said he had tried to access Canadian data concerning alien contact and had been told it was higher than his security clearance!

Space travel through the vast distances of space is impossible. The vast distances of space are a safe guard meant expressly to keep humanity within his own solar system.

All research into the UFO and the abduction phenomena indicates an evil influence.

After all, how many times would a space alien capable of interstellar travel have to abduct a person and perform sexual experiments to know what makes one tick?

US NUKES AND UFOS

Six former U.S. Air Force officers and one former enlisted man
gave testimony of UFOs at a press conference at the National
Press Club in Washington, DC, on Sept. 27, 2010, during which
airmen who had been stationed at different nuclear bases around
the country said that they witnessed UFOs that were able to disable the nuclear weapons.

"Nobody was injured, and I don't consider it an attack, but it certainly was a national security incident and something the Air Force
said has never happened in their official policy documents," said
[4]Robert Salas, a former U.S. Air Force nuclear launch officer.

He further stated he was on duty one clear, dark night when
glowing red orbs appeared over Malmstrom AFB in Montana. At
the same time, the weapons were disabled.

"[44]Richard M. Dolan, author of *UFOs and the National Security
State*, described in his work "one of the most extraordinary events
in the history of military-UFO encounters."

A topside security guard and flight security controller with the
Oscar Flight Launch Control Center (LCC) "saw a star-like object
zigzagging high above him. Soon, a larger and closer light also appeared and acted in similar fashion."

---

[4]   UFOs and Nukes: Extraordinary Encounters at Nuclear Weapons Sites

The NCO was quickly alerted. Captain Robert Salas was at work below ground in the launch control center when the NCO called him with the news.

"Great," Salas said skeptically. "You just keep watching them and let me know if they get any closer."

When the NCO called Salas again, the fear in his voice was evident as he described the strange, red, glowing object that hovered outside the front gate. Guards had drawn their weapons and were waiting on orders.

Forty-three percent of Americans believe in UFOs.

Not sure what was going on at the front gate, Salas approached his commander, Lt. Fred Meiwald, and explained what had been happening.

An alarm suddenly went off. Salas and Meiwald were startled to see the "No-Go" light for one of the missiles flash on. "No-Go" means that the missile was inoperable. That was followed by more "No-Go" lights as five to seven more missiles went down. At that moment, national security was compromised. But as suddenly as they had come, the mysterious red lights left.

Twenty miles away at the Echo-Flight launch facilities, it was happening all over again. Like Salas, First Lt. Walter Figel was on duty at his station. His first clue that something was not right was when the "No-Go" light flashed on for one of the missiles. Concerned, he picked up the phone to call the missile site. Was there a scheduled missile maintenance of which he was not aware?

The security guard who took the call told him that maintenance had not yet taken place. He went on to describe a UFO seen hovering over the site.

Figel was as skeptical as Salas had been at first. However, something odd and unforeseen was definitely happening, as ten more missiles suddenly and mysteriously entered a "No-Go" status.

The UFO appearance was witnessed by the maintenance and security personnel. In his book, Dolan reports that "the missiles were down for the greater part of a day. The air force investigation included full-scale tests on-site, as well as laboratory tests at the Boeing Company's Seattle plant. No cause for the shutdown could be found."

According to the Boeing engineering chief, "There was no technical explanation that could account for the event."

These kinds of incidents seem to be all too common with rumored events in North America, Great Britain, Russia, and Israel. A 2000 poll found forty-three percent of Americans believe in UFOs. There is an old saying: where there is smoke, there is fire. I would look for greater government disclosure and more whistleblowers to come forth with incredible stories.

STARGATES

In some witchcraft and Wiccan systems, the Watchers are beings who guard portals that link worlds together.

WITHIN SUCH SYSTEMS THEY ARE viewed as a spiritual race, a set of deities, or as spirits of the four elements. Some Italian witches believe that the Grigori (Watchers) are such an ancient race. The Watchers are known by many names including the Old Ones and the Dread Lords of the Outer Spaces. We know them as the fallen angels of Rahab. Sometimes they transverse into our realm through portals—openings for interdimensional visitations from other realities or dimensions that coexist separately alongside our own. Both good and bad angels can produce openings.

Are there examples of these *openings?* Yes, and the most well known is Jacob's ladder, but the most awesome and colorful are when God chooses to make His presence known. Oh, I might add that there are many portals these days as time nears its end, and many have become deceived by these portals. Some enthusiasts of the supernatural look for orbs, doorways, or portals, wishing to contact beings from these other dimensions. Believe me when I say not all beings in these dimensions are friendly! There are some in the realms who have worked since Lucifer's fall to destroy humanity, transversing these realms using openings to deceive humanity— sometimes taking the shape of metallic disks. They often mock God by appearing as messengers. The question should always be, however, messengers of whom?

In Psalms there is a statement that God "rode upon a cherub" and flew. This is elaborated upon further, as shown in this remark- able revelation.

45 Then the earth shook and trembled; the foundations also of the hills moved and were shaken... There went up a smoke out of [God's] nostrils, and fire out of his mouth devoured: coals were kindled by it.

He bowed the heavens also, and came down: and darkness was under his feet. He made darkness his secret place; his pavilion round about him was dark waters and thick clouds of the skies.

When dimensions are transversed, there are all sorts of physical manifestations such as brightness, thick clouds, hail stones, thunder, lightnings, and sparks. This physical manifestation of thick clouds is the most common phenomenon surrounding God's appearance. Four different times these "thick clouds" are mentioned in the Scriptures (Job 22:14, 26:8, Ps. 18:11 and 18:12) in relation to the transversing of His throne into this dimension.

In Joel 2:2 and Zephaniah 1:5, we see that thick clouds and darkness will surround God's throne on the Day of Judgment.

These thick clouds are often followed by loud noises such as one might expect to hear when an airplane or space shuttle breaks the sound barrier.

46 The LORD also thundered in the heavens, and the Highest gave his voice (Ps. 18:12).

The above verse is a harrowing description of the noises that accompany God's throne.

Sometimes these same noises will accompany portal events; they are not exclusive to the Lord's travel but might also be heard when lesser beings transverse into our dimension. Upon [47]Mount Sinai many thunders, lightnings, fire, smoke, and a thick cloud descended as God's throne approached—so much so that the ground quaked and trembled. [48]Moses reported, "So terrible was the sight that I exceedingly feared and quaked!"

This is a celebrated picture of God's throne opening as a portal event into our dimension.

[49]Enoch described traveling through a portal. *Behold, in that vision clouds and a mist invited me; agitated stars and flashes of lightning impelled and pressed me forwards, while winds in the vision assisted my flight, accelerating my progress* (Enoch 14:9).

In his book *Chariots of the Gods,* Erich von Däniken based his entire hypothesis that the Earth was visited by aliens upon a single passage in Ezekiel. Little did he know that this was merely a description of God's throne traveling from one realm to another. He went on to postulate that aliens gave the technologies of the ancient civilizations to them. He was right about the fact that ancient technologies were not inherent in man but wrong upon the assumption of space-traveling aliens.

The speed of light prohibits matter from traveling beyond its limits in our realm; it's a sort of stop sign, if you will. The Creator built into the system automatic stops such as the speed of light. The reason? To stop the spread of sin and corruption.

Humanity limited to below the speed of light would never gain entry to other worlds, though he might imagine such worlds in his mind. It seems ancient man knew this limitation and in the building of the Tower of Babel may have been looking for a way to circumvent it.

Portals and the attempt to create them is nothing new. Humanity has been about trying to create them since the Tower of Babel. However, the legitimizing the search of such is entirely new.

Now emerging figures in Christendom are seeking to create openings. There seems to be a rush to see who can outdo whom. What once was understood to be forbidden is now fast becoming legitimized by left-wing Christians. What they expect to step out of these event horizons is an interesting question.

Even now some parts of the country have groups seeking to open portals, thinking only good beings can come through the opening! They might be surprised!

Many are familiar with television's acclaimed *Stargate* series where the stars transport through shimmering openings left behind by "the old ones." This theme is further developed into good and bad ancients. There truly are old ones, but not ancients of the *Stargate* variety, and the real ones are all bad.

When a portal ingress activates, time can be suspended.

Dimensional doorways are opened as is often seen in UFO encounters that stop time. A vortex, cloud, or haze will appear. Many UFO sightings follow this pattern and are connected with these portal-opening events.

Portals are what they are: *openings into this dimension from another dimension.* The question is, for what purpose and what might one expect to come through?

Lucifer has from the beginning attempted to keep humanity in the dark, destroying any true information.

The Book of Enoch, The Book of Jubilees, and the Book of Giants are examples of fallen angels destroying information about themselves.

Our history is filled with the noble who have suffered at the hands of the fallen angels. There have been many who have given their lives to further mankind's knowledge of these events; even now in our time many are giving their lives in an effort to inform mankind of the story.

CONSPIRACY

Webster describes paranoia as a belief in delusions of danger and persecution. However, I propose that if the danger is real and the evidence credible, then it cannot be delusional.

THE CONSPIRACY EMBRACES INDIVIDUALS AND organizations in what might be called an attempt to alter the path of mankind along a predetermined way for the benefit of a special group. It is a master plan that connects individuals, corporations, banks, foundations, and organizations to a hidden agenda, usually one of global dominance. Individuals and organizations such as the United Nations, the Bilderbergers, the Lucis Trust, the Club of Rome, the Carnegies, Freemasonry, the Illuminati, the Council on Foreign Relations, the Trilateral Commission, and Jekyll Island, Georgia, along with its establishment of the Federal Reserve, have been implicated in global conspiracies.

Conspiracies generally have as their main theme a group aiming to bring about changes that will usher in a new era of world order through dominance by a one-world government.

This one world government will be the tool of the Antichrist. He will have a network allied with him, a system that with its powerful influence over the world's monetary and political systems will contribute to his ultimate world control. There is, however, a far greater conspiracy connecting the Antichrist to a one-world government, which is truly unknown but of greater importance. Most global conspiracies are segmented into one small group operating here or there. However, I will show you what is behind all of these conspiracies of globalization.

There is ample evidence that there has been and is now a global conspiracy through an unknown number of members all sharing the same vision. Those constituents are not normal people but the fallen angels themselves.

While people are saying, "peace and security," destruction will come on them suddenly (1 Thess. 5:3).

The Middle East peace process is gaining momentum, championed by scientists, economists, media, businessmen, and heads of state from all around the world. Little do they know that they are playing into the Dark Lord's hand and setting the stage for the arrival of the Antichrist!

In the days leading up to World War II, Winston Churchill brought a message which was contrary to the beliefs of the prevailing society, which at the time wanted assurance that the world had obtained peace and safety. Lord Chamberlain, the British Prime Minister, upon his return from Munich waved a piece of paper signed by Hitler and Mussolini, saying, "I bring you peace, peace in our time." The whole nation was ecstatic, thinking that he had saved them from war. Not so Churchill. He knew this for what it was: a foretaste of tyranny.

Churchill's message, which went unheeded with most Brits because they believed him to be a war monger, proved instrumental in the changes that British society was to face a few years later as World War II set the world aflame.

Shakespeare once said, "all the world's a stage, and all the men and women merely players." We can look back and see that Winston Churchill played his part upon the world's stage and at a crucial moment brought a message of paramount importance. While Great Britain slept, Churchill warned again and again of the dangers lurking in the darkness. He warned unceasingly of the danger of Germany's rearming itself. Day and night while Great Britain slept, Germany continued to produce arms while verbally espousing peace.

> **"[He] who controls the MONEY can control the WORLD."**

In these troubled times, will the world continue to sleep as the approaching juggernaut of the Apocalypse gets closer and closer, or will it awake? Sadly, there is no indication that the world or its leaders are cognizant of this looming time of derision. [50]In fact, the world will be eating and drinking until the day that the trumpet sounds.

[51]*And he shall send his angels with a great sound of a trumpet, and they shall gather together his elect from the four winds, from one end of heaven to the other* (Matt. 24:30).

Still Churchill spoke of impending tyranny and subjugation of the masses, as many ancient prophecies warn of the coming end of the world. Awake, awake, for the time is short!

The conspirators are an all-powerful, evil force manipulating lesser actors while they themselves stay in the background. However, this cloaking will not always be a part of the play, for as the end gets nearer and nearer, they will reveal themselves.

ONE WORLD GOVERNMENT

These fallen angels control a network of foundations, banks, oil cartels, corporations, and associations controlling the greater part of the global economy.

ALL THE KINGDOMS OF THE world will become a one-world government. Now with this in mind, let us look at an ancient text.

*The Dark Prince takes the Lord up into an exceeding high mountain, and shows him all the **kingdoms of the world**, and the glory of them; And says to him, All these **kingdoms of the world** will I give you, if you will fall down and worship me* (Matt. 4:8–9, paraphrased).

In order for Lucifer to have control over the empires, he must first have political and financial control of national leaders. Through tyranny, bribery, and control of the money systems, he has been able to manipulate and influence political leaders throughout the centuries.

As Henry Kissinger once said, "[He] who controls the MONEY can control the WORLD."

The fallen angels have from time immortal been the real power brokers.

The fallen angels have used the Council on Foreign Relations and the financial powers behind it to promote their "New World Order." The fallen angels believe in the concept of a government controlled by the elite (themselves), and they are working tenaciously toward the overthrow of the Constitution and American sovereignty.

Through the Council on Foreign Relations, they attempt to direct national governments as well as corporations through the control of grants, education, and media. To quote William Blasé, "The Council on Foreign Relations is the promotional arm of the ruling elite." The ruling elite are fallen angels!

A casual perusal of the membership list of present and past presidents, congressional representatives, newscasters, and bankers who have participated in this organization will send chills up anyone's spine. Why are there so many power players in one world government ideology?

In *The New World Order*, Pat Robertson states that "the elite realized that America would not join any scheme for world government without a change in public opinion." This led to the organization of the Council on Foreign Relations, whose purpose was to change public opinion.

Admiral Chester Ward, a member of the Council on Foreign Relations, revealed its inner workings in a 1975 book he co-wrote with Phyllis Schlafly called *Kissinger on the Couch*. In it, he states that "the most powerful cliques in this elitist group have but one objective in common: they want to bring about the surrender of the sovereignty and national independence of the United States."

The Council on Foreign Relations is only one of the many organizations working to bring about a one-world government. The most dangerous and the one with the greatest impact upon the average American is the Federal Reserve.

That there are Dark Lords behind the halls of power has been attested to by many in a position to know.

Established on Jekyll Island, Georgia, around the turn of the century, the Federal Reserve is a privately-owned organization of member banks and individuals.

It makes its own policies and is not subject to Congress. With the Stock Market Crash, the Great Depression, and numerous recessions, it is obvious the Federal Reserve produces nothing but inflation, debt, and the devaluation of the dollar. Some of the major shareholders are the Lehman Brothers, Goldman and Sachs, Rockefeller, and the Rothschild's. The remaining balance of stock is owned by commercial member banks.

What is going on here? Are the people who are concerned about these things simply being neurotic or conniving theorists, determined to see conspiracies around every corner? No! *That there are Dark Lords behind the halls of power has been attested to by many in a position to know.*

Felix Frankfurter (Supreme Court Justice, 1939-1962)

"The real rulers in Washington are invisible and exercise power from behind the scenes."

President Franklin Roosevelt (Nov. 21, 1933)

"The real truth of the matter is, as you and I know, that a financial element in the large centers has owned the government ever since the days of Andrew Jackson."

Senator William Jenner (Feb. 23, 1954)

"Outwardly we have a Constitutional government. We have operating within our government and political system another body representing another form of government, a bureaucratic elite which believes our Constitution is outmoded."

Baron M.A. Rothschild

"Give me control over a nation's currency and I care not who makes its laws."

Congressman Louis McFadden (1920-31)

"When the Federal Reserve Act was passed, the people of these United States did not perceive that a world banking system was being set up here. A super-state controlled by international bankers and industrialists...acting together to enslave the world.

"Every effort has been made by the Fed to conceal its powers but the truth is–the Fed has usurped the government."

At last, the Illuminati must be mentioned. They are international bankers with agents infiltrating most other secret societies. The Illuminati became a dirty word when its doings became known. The organization was banned in 1785, but most writers feel it just went underground.

Jekyll Island, with its establishment of the Federal Reserve and with its founders being international bankers, lends some credit to the Illuminati conspiracy still being alive and well. Some of the biggest names in the country attended the meeting on Jekyll Island that spawned the Federal Reserve. I wonder who among them were fallen angels.

THE RETURN OF THE NEPHILIM

NOW I WILL SHARE A personal experience. There was a brisk chill in the air on the moonless night late one November when I saw for the first time what I believe to be one of the children of the fallen angels.

As was my custom, I donned my walking shoes and grabbed my dog Star's leash. It was time for her walk. As we began our walk, it seemed like any other normal nighttime excursion. Star and I headed down the driveway as usual.

Since we live off the beaten path, our driveway is surrounded by local wildlife, and we have a large stand of mountain laurel about half way down the drive. Not in any particular hurry, we took our time walking at a leisurely pace.

No sooner had we approached this stand of mountain laurel than Star began to pull as she does when she sees an animal, normally a quail or rabbit she wants to give chase to. But as she began to pull, she acted in an unusual way. At first I thought she was spooked by what she must have smelled.

Something part human, part dog stood and looked at me from behind a large tree surrounded by bushes.

As I stood there wondering what she heard or sensed, a cold chill began to run down my back, and I had the sensation of being watched. I was armed with a fairly good-sized flashlight, so I panned it in an arch ahead of me. I wasn't prepared for what my light fell on.

Something part human, part dog stood and looked at me from behind a large tree surrounded by bushes. The creature and I stared at each other. Neither of us moved for what seemed like several seconds. Then suddenly, the creature was gone! I shined the light around the area. Finding only empty darkness, I began to believe I had hallucinated.

Quickly, I tugged on Star's leash, but there was no need. She was as eager to be gone as I was. Behind the heaven of my locked door, it was still a while before I could calm my insides, although I felt completely that God was in control.

My wife later decided to venture outside. She did not see any creature but said there was fear in the air so thick that she thought she could cut it with a knife, the kind of fear that makes the hair rise on the nape of your neck!

The Antichrist could be a prime example of a nephilim born to look normal.

We talked over our experience together and decided that God had allowed this in order to call us into battle and to spread the news. What had only been a mere thesis became intensely real as I stood, staring at a creature that I had only read about. What had been a desire to study and write now became an alarm to be sounded.

Certain Egyptian hieroglyphs and Greek deities have an intriguing likeness to what I saw on this dark evening, especially the mythical satyr.

I came to the conclusion that the creature I saw was a nephilim. It was about six feet tall and had a face resembling that of a dog.

Later, I learned the international reporting agency for UFO's had posted a sighting that same evening. These half-animal hybrids have been seen by others in connection with UFO's, so one appearing in my area came as no surprise.

One word of caution: UFO's and their doings in every way resemble demonic activity and should be avoided. Many researchers who are coming to this conclusion are creditable scientists. Their warnings should be heeded. Do not attempt to contact UFO's, for they are malevolent and could involve an abduction phenomenon.

Alien abductions were taking place in Genesis 6, and more importantly, prophetically speaking, these abductions (fornications) are still going on today!

In both Matthew 24:37 and Luke 17:26-30, Jesus stated that the end times would be "like the days of Noah."

What was happening in the days of Noah? Fallen angels (Sons of God) were fornicating with humans, creating hybrids. These hybrids were giants in those times.

Luke 17:26–30 especially leads me to draw this conclusion because not only are the days of Noah mentioned, but Sodom and Gomorrah are mentioned in the same paragraph as well.

> **The Evil Ones will continue deceiving governments of the world, eventually compelling full disclosure of alien or "star god" (fallen angel) contact.**

Matthew 24:37

But as the days of Noah were, so shall also the coming of the Son of man be.

Luke 17:26-30

And as it was in the days of Noe (Noah), so shall it be also in the days of the Son of man. They did eat, they drank, they married wives, they were given in marriage, until the day that Noe entered into the ark, and the flood came, and destroyed them all.

Likewise, also as it was in the days of Lot; they did eat, they drank, they bought, they sold, they planted, they builded; But the same day that Lot went out of Sodom it rained fire and brimstone from heaven, and destroyed them all. Even thus shall it be in the day when the Son of man is revealed.

To confirm the above statements, recently there has come to the forefront of the news a woman claiming to have been abducted and given birth to nephilim. Now another five women have come forward to claim the same thing.

[52] These women claim that the fallen angels are working to fix the problem of gigantism in order to be indistinguishable from normal people. This claim cannot be taken lightly. More is being

revealed about the nephilim as we get closer to the end of time. Could the fallen angels be seducing the military, perhaps trading technology they have been creating for thousands of years, for the opportunity to breed with women and create hybrid nephilims as many claim? Think of this: if the fallen angels wanted to breed with women, wouldn't they offer technology in return for "genetic experiments," perhaps in order to produce indistinguishable nephilim?

However, I think this is only part of the puzzle. I think both giants and nephilim, which are indistinguishable from normal people, will be born. The Antichrist could be a prime example of a nephilim born to look normal. Now, who do you suppose his father will be? Brainstorming led me to this plausible answer: the Antichrist will be fathered by no other than Lucifer!

THE PLAYERS

Few know of the conspiracy, which has brought us to this apex of human history.

THE CONSPIRATORS HAVE A LONG and dark history. Their history spans eons of time. Once they were the players upon the grand stage of the cosmos. Once they colonized worlds, traded among the stars, and held high and exalted places.

Now they hide among us, the ever surging mass of humanity, forever manipulating us to our own demise. They having been with us at every turning point of history, working a plan known only to them.

Occasionally, one of their numbers will come to the forefront of the world arena. When this happens, the world shivers, and their names are forever added to the list of the infamous.

Where did men such as Hitler, Stalin, Mao Tse Tung, Kim Jong, Paul Pot, Edi Amin, Attila the Hun, Gingiss Kahn, Mohammad, Caesar, King Herod, Saladin, and Osama Bin Laden come from? Men such as these suddenly appear upon the world's stage with no real genealogy and just as suddenly disappear. Could any of these be Dark Lords, appearing as people? For this is exactly what you would expect to see: powerful men appearing with no past and disappearing just as easily.

These fallen angels are the true conspirators, and they are the true power brokers. This conspiracy is ongoing, and its members are alive and well. The Evil Ones will continue deceiving governments of the world, eventually compelling full disclosure of alien or "star god" (fallen angel) contact.

It also seems that the human race still suffers from the ancient interaction between the fallen angels (*beney 'elohim*) and the "daughters of men." It can be seen today.

The genetic defects can be seen when a child is born with six toes or six fingers. The doctors remove them, and no more thought is given to it.

Pictures, rock carvings, and statues from all over the world depict hands with six fingers and feet with six toes, from Egypt to the [53]Three Rivers area of Southeast New Mexico, where there are over 20,000 petroglyphs (rock carvings) of six-fingered hands.

Six toes and six fingers were the ancient caricature of corrupt DNA! All nephilim and elouid have this sexdactyly. An example of this was seen in a battle that took place millennia ago in Gath.

And then there was the war at Gath that featured a hulking **giant** *who had* **twenty-four fingers** *and* **toes***, six on each hand and foot—yet another from the* **clan of giants** (1 Chron. 20:6).

Sexdactyly is reported in two out of one thousand births.

A dominant gene causes it. In fact, there are small populations of localized sexdactyly rumored to be all over the world, and this is part of the hybrid DNA left in the gene pool.

There is mounting evidence in our modern times (End Times) that the intervention of fallen angels is growing greater and greater again!

This is a harbinger of the mark of the beast (666), meaning that the Antichrist will be a product of the fallen angels, perhaps the Prince of the fallen angels himself. He may even have six fingers and six toes, although doctors might have removed these.

Fallen angels can shape-shift (borrowed from *Star Trek*) into human beings and are able to have intercourse with humans or animals, and this causes genetic defects in the hybrid. The union of these fallen angels with humans produces children that are genetically different in many ways. The main differences are those of gigantism and the irregularity of six fingers and six toes, but there are also

Sexdactyly is reported in two out of one thousand births.

other overlooked irregularities such as extreme intelligence and psychic abilities.

We owe the pyramids and great structures the world over to this extreme intelligence, as well as horrendous things such as cannibalism and human sacrifice.

Some celebrities are rumored to have had six fingers and/or six toes at birth, which is a genetic marker of gigantism and past involvement of the fallen angels in their DNA. Not that they're hybrids, but they certainly carry a corrupted gene from their descendants. Oprah Winfrey and Marilyn Monroe are two of those who have been touched by such a rumor.

A not as well-known example of a corrupted gene is that of Zhang Ruifang, a woman living in China who in 2010 was 101 years old. A small genetic corruption somewhere in her lineage has caused a horn to grow on her forehead in her old age. Those who know her call it a devil's horn. The horn on Zhang Ruifang has grown to six centimeters in length, and another horn is forming on the opposite side of her forehead. The horn is composed of the same material found in fingernails. However, this is more proof that the fallen angels have corrupted the human genome.

CONCLUSION

Normally, conspirators have the expectation of achieving their goals during their own lifetime.

BUT THIS ISN'T THE CASE with the fallen angels. They operate only on a long-range plan. Whether it will take scores of years or centuries, they are timeless. They can wait it out. They are dedicated only to evil and the overthrow of nation states to create a one-world government.

Some of these conspirators are not human; they are fallen angels. They have crossed over and taken flesh upon themselves and are controlling the world's plunge to judgment.

The final phases of the one-world government inspired by these conspirators (fallen angels) will consist of the Antichrist at its supreme head.

Some have gathered personal fortunes so large as to be beyond our ability to measure them. Fortunes stolen from the world's smalls and greats are amassed in shielded bank accounts owned by shell corporations. These fallen angels' personal wealth is larger than some countries. They control private armies, and they are hidden among the masses, seemingly unnoticed by the common person.

Some fallen angels control drug cartels, some control countries, and some are so well known as to be thought human. Their capacity for evil is immense but measured. They are working toward an end. The Hitlers of the world we can well imagine in our minds, but what about the owner of that private island you happen to know about? What about your banker? What about your neighbor?

HE WAS CAST OUT INTO THE EARTH

And there was war in heaven: Michael and his angels fought against the dragon; and the dragon fought and his angels, And prevailed not; neither was their place found any more in heaven. And the great dragon was cast out, that old serpent, called the Devil, and Satan, which deceiveth the whole world: he was cast out into the earth, and his angels were cast out with him (Rev 12:7-9) (KJV).

The Dark Lords will be cast out of the spiritual places into the physical. What this means is that the spiritual, fallen angels will be forced to take physical bodies! Woe to the inhabitants of the earth!

Why theologians have not seen this is a wonder. The times are dark indeed and getting darker. I hope all who read this will prepare themselves for the encroaching darkness–if there is any way to prepare. That the devil will make war on the saints is no doubt, but how many have thought they would be looking at fallen angels?

I may be a Winston Churchill in this alarm, but alarm I must. The day comes soon when the Dark Lord will make war face to face with the saints.

EPILOGUE

There is upon tomorrow's doorstep a deluge of divine wrath to be expected universally to overwhelm this wicked world.

The great day of the LORD is near, it is near, and hasteth greatly, even the voice of the day of the LORD: the mighty man shall cry there bitterly. That day is a day of wrath, a day of trouble and distress, a day of wasteness and desolation, a day of darkness and gloominess, a day of clouds and thick darkness (Zeph. 1:14–15).

WILL YOU PREPARE?

Thus did Noah; according to all that God commanded him, so did he (Gen. 6:22) (KJV).

Will you prepare for the coming deluge of divine wrath? When the Great Flood consumed the old world, there was only one, Noah, who was prepared.

Will you be prepared to save yourself, your family, your neighbor from this day?

Everything that Noah had forewarned the people about came to pass. I have forewarned you of the approaching footsteps of the Horsemen of the Apocalypse and the soon return of the nephilim.

Do not fail to prepare and build an ark for yourself and your family. Delay and you may be incapable of offering salvation to those who would knock upon your door. Begin to prepare now.

The Russian bear is in a slumber, but he shall put off his slumber and awake. Woe unto the inhabitances of the world, for he shall arise and be hungry.

You begin to hear what seems like thousands of military-operator conversations, and as you listen more closely, you begin to hear news commentators saying one thing and another. As you strain to hear the words, you can barely make it out, but you hear, "the national power grid" and "virus," then a momentary break, after which you begin to hear multiple explosions.

Many different explosions come one after another, followed by a pause of a few minutes before you hear the words (as an announce-ment), "Ladies and gentlemen, the president of the United States."

The West is not expecting a nuclear attack by Iran and certainly not from the Russian declawed bear, but these cannot be ruled out. Russia continues to spend, by one author's estimate, an excess of six billion dollars a year on "civil defense."

You remember the bomb shelter! Russia diligently continues to spend on building bomb shelters. Russia has even built an entire city below the Ural Mountains for shelter while telling the world their bankrupt. Do they know something we don't?

Unknown is the fact that many countries and individuals are preparing for the coming apocalypse. The rich, the powerful, and of course the military of most countries are [54]digging in the mountains, the most celebrated of which is Cheyenne Mountain, the home of

North American Aerospace Defense Command. As it is written, they *hid themselves in the dens and in the rocks of the mountains* (Rev. 6:17).

What would be the earliest clue of an all-out attack? Why of course—explosions in the stratosphere! The sky would light up with brightness, and momentarily a ring similar to a halo would be seen.

Suddenly, an outage of all electric power and communications would be noticed. Automobiles would even be affected; they would cease to run. Anything not shielded from an EMP (electromagnetic pulse), a burst of electromagnetic radiation resulting from a nuclear explosion at high altitude, would be severely damaged. Even high voltage power stations would be knocked completely off line, and it is not known when or even if they could be brought back.

Radio and television stations would quit transmitting because of circuit overloads (over-voltages in their microprocessors). An EMP attack would totally disable all stations across the [55]United States. These EMP effects would be the result of submarine-launched missiles exploding in the stratosphere, specifically designed to produce electromagnetic pulse (EMP).

These submarine-launched missiles would be the first warning of an all-out attack. These bursts would make no sound whatsoever because of the great height from which they are detonated in the stratosphere; however, within a few minutes (approximately fifteen) other explosions would be heard or felt from different locations as other missiles take out high value targets such as missile silos. This is the beginning of sorrows.

THE WATCHMAN

The labels *prophet* and *visionary* are highly subjective; a person considered an authentic prophet by some will be considered a false prophet by others—or at least abnormal by modern scholars.

However, in a society that is out of control, which creates movies such as *Skyline* and games such as Dungeons and Dragons, you should not find these writings unusual.

A prophet as an individual does not fit into society; he ridicules its assumptions, its self-righteousness, and its lack of moral direction. He rants at the world as if it were a slum. But if such sensitivity to evil is hilarious, what should we think of the assumptions, complacency, and the world's lack of ethical bearing that the prophet bewails?

The prophet is intent on intensifying responsibility, is intolerant of excuse, and is disdainful of pretense and self-piety.

His tone and mannerisms are frequently disturbing, even horrid. His mannerisms and tone are designed to shock rather than to calm and console.

The prophet challenges the holy, revered, and cherished beliefs of the institutions and the community. The prophet knows and understands that religion distorts God, and that the clergy has committed perjury in its toleration of moral ambiguity.

The prophet hates the middle of the road. The prophet is a black and white thinker, one-sided, strange, and an unbearable extremist to family and friends. A prophet faces intolerant authorities in established religion.

The things that horrified the prophets of old are now daily occurrences, so how can the prophet remain quiet? Howbeit, there are many pretenders who predict peace, prosperity, and a God who will give America another chance if America will but repent.

America will be given no second chance. I find this admonition distasteful and a burden, one which stigmatizes and conjures the thought that I might be a madman. But speak I must, warn I will.

They hate him who reproves in the gate; they abhor him who speaks the truth (Amos 5:10).

A prophet more than anything else is a watchman. A watchman must be alert and wary. Today many have failed their duty to warn of impending destruction and imminent danger as the Tribulation draws near. They are asleep at their posts, unable to see the approaching holocaust. The self-proclaimed watchmen of today are bought off with the luxuries of life. They desire a better tomorrow for themselves and their children. A vigilant watchman warns of imminent danger. His duty is to warn of impending ruin.

Ezekiel 33:1–7 says, *Again the word of the Lord came to me, saying, "Son of man, speak to the children of your people, and say to them: 'When I bring the sword upon a land, and the people of the land take a man from their territory and make him their watchman, when he sees the sword coming upon the land, if he blows the trumpet and warns the people, then whoever hears the sound of the trumpet and does not take warning, if the sword comes and takes him away, his blood shall be on his own head. He heard the sound of the trumpet, but did not take warning; his blood shall be on himself. But he who takes warning will save his life.*

But if the watchman sees the sword coming, and does not blow the trumpet, and the people are not warned, and the sword comes and takes any person from among them, he is taken away in his iniquity; but his blood I will require at the watchman's hand.' So, you son of man: I have made you a watchman for the house of Israel; therefore you shall hear a word from My mouth and warn them for Me."

When the Lord spoke to Ezekiel, he understood the duty of the watchman. He as well as people of that time knew the consequence of a faithful guard, because watchmen were always in the watchtowers of the citadels. They were ever on guard, scanning the horizon for an approaching enemy. The townspeople could sleep at night knowing that a watchman was on the wall and if attacked, the watchman would warn them and awake them. A faithful watchman knows that the enemy's attack can come at any moment and is therefore vigilant.

This utter darkness has been developing since the beginning of time and has been foretold in prophecy. This second Dark Age is approaching as we sleep. We are marrying and partying like no other generation. The Roaring Twenties has taken a back seat to the "gayness" of this generation. We have taken our pleasures as country has risen against country with slaughters and war crimes; we have turned the music up a little louder and pacified ourselves with the thought that tomorrow would somehow be better. However, we are like men drowning in quicksand. We hide our heads and cover our eyes, hoping it will all go away. Tomorrow will arrive as a bright sun-shining day.

Like so many, I have at times chanted the same mantra until the evening I came face-to-face with a nephilim. What had moments earlier been merely theology and a belief became vividly real as I stood staring at a creature that easily could tear me limb from limb. My desire to study and write about this subject became instead a desire to sound the alarm and warn others.

Recently a neighbor's home caught fire. A stranger driving by saw smoke and stopped. He got out of his car and pounded on the homeowner's door until he awakened. The homeowner was grateful to be alerted to the danger. My hope is that, as the awakened neighbor, you will be grateful to read this warning.

I have been asked how I would react if I again came face-to-face with a nephilim. First, I will have to admit I was not afraid. I don't know why, other than I had confidence that God would protect me. I was overwhelmed more with curiosity than with fear but exercised common sense in returning home and locking the door.

How should someone else respond? It depends entirely upon their relationship to Christ. A born-again believer is given power over evil in the name of Jesus.

> *Behold, I give unto you power to tread on serpents and scorpions, and over all the power of the enemy: and nothing shall by any means hurt you* (Luke 10:19).

I believe this monster would have been entirely subject to my command had I commanded it to leave in the name of Jesus. Should I not have been a Christian, I would have wished for a very big gun!

AUTHOR'S BIOGRAPHY

I WAS BORN IN A small, insignificant town in the southern part of the USA, so far south that they had to pipe in the sunshine!

I was born in the month of April into a family of twelve in South Georgia on an island called Cumberland. April in the south warms as it recovers from mild winters and takes on a new life as azaleas bloom, porpoises frolic, and wild horses give birth to new colts.

Cumberland is a wonderful place with its tidal pools, abundant wildlife, untouched sand dunes, deep forests, and history. Heck, around the turn of the century, we even had a bear! I'll not mention the alligators other than to say we had our share of them. But they're about as worthless as the sharks, of which Christmas Creek has an ample supply. My siblings and I explored the beaches and the forests on a daily basis.

Each of us learned to swim at the ripe young age of five by being thrown off the dock with a rope tied around the waist. Our father thought it was of the utmost importance that we learn to swim. I guess he was right, seeing that we lived on an island! Perhaps the training method was a little harsh (I would not recommend it), but it was effective.

Somewhere around the time I had reached eight or so years of age, I experienced my first vision. One evening as I returned to my bedroom, a wall disappeared.

Where the wall had been was a man sitting upon a stage. He sat in a chair at the edge of the stage, putting his hands upon the heads of those passing by beneath him.

As I watched these people walk beneath him, he laid his hands upon them. I realized that the man was me, just older! It was obvious that I was in some kind of ministry. I thought all of this very unusual, because I had never seen anything like this. All I knew about ministry at this time was what I learned in the Methodist Church. You can rest assured nothing like this was going on in the Methodist Church in the 1960s.

I was by definition a tenacious child, but about what I did not know. In the early 1970s upon turning twelve, I took my first steps into business ownership; I built a shop in my parents' backyard and began repairing lawnmowers. It was a great income for a teenager, perhaps too good. As most coming-of-age young people, sin lurked at my doorstep. By 1977, I was an aspiring teenage alcoholic, complete with blackouts. Even at this tender age, the world had shown its web of deceit, lies, and drama.

I will always be indebted to a caring science teacher for his introducing me to the living Christ. As most of us have heard of Christ, I had heard, having grown up, as I mentioned, in church.

However, this humble man was the first person I had met who really seemed to have a relationship with this Jesus the God/Man. I am sure there must have been others like him with whom I had contact, but none that I knew seemed to have the kind of feelings exemplifying a real relationship with Jesus. I began to talk with him between classes.

On one particular day, I meditated on a text of scripture in Ecclesiastes.

Vanity of vanity, saith the Preacher, vanity of vanities, all is vanity (Ecclesiastes 1:2).

I was moved by a war of sorts that seemed to be going on within me; it was as if evil was determined to drag my soul along with it. It literally was evil vying within me for my soul. It had the opposite effect. You could say that it "scared the hell out of me." I returned the next day to talk again with my teacher.

I eagerly waited for the class to end, knowing I then would have time to speak about the struggle I had felt the night before in my soul. When the moment arrived, I dashed from my desk to where he stood.

I began to relate the struggle I had felt, and he asked me if I would pray and receive Christ. I wanted to but could not speak. I had become dumb; I was not able to open my mouth to speak in any manner! Seeming to understand this strange occurrence, he pointed directly at me and spoke commandingly to a devil, one that I could not see. He told the devil to go in the name of Jesus!

Immediately I cried at the top of my voice, "Jesus!"

I knew not what to say, only crying out to Jesus, the one I knew who alone could rescue me from the war that had only moments ago rendered me unable to speak. As I heard myself cry out, I became aware of the darkness within my soul. It was as if I was looking inside of myself as some kind of spectator.

As I surveyed the vastness of this darkness, I became cognizant of the fact that in the middle of this vast darkness, there was a pinpoint of light beginning to expand at an ever-increasing velocity until it appeared as a supernova and burst forth out of every part of my being, leaving my extremities at what seemed to me to be the speed of light. I staggered a few feet and recovered my composure. I was stunned.

I certainly had no point of reference for what I had just experienced. The years to come would, of course, show the vast changes that had occurred. I no longer was an alcoholic—or an addict of any kind—from that moment forward. I later learned that the "old man" had died and the "new man" had been born. I had been "born again" and would never be the same.

Now, nearly four decades later, I can say it was the defining moment of my life.

ADDENDUM

WHERE DID ANGELS COME FROM?

There is no easy answer to this question, but let's give it a try.

You alone are Yahweh. You made the heavens, even the highest heavens, and all their starry host, the earth and all that is on it, the seas and all that is in them. You gave life to everything, and the multitudes of heaven worship you (Nehemiah 9:6).

Angels might be humanoids, composed of a physical and spiritual nature. Perhaps before the creation of the world, in the eons past, they were only physical. This would mean humans and angels are just on different levels of ascension.

There are some scriptural references indicating that other entities in the universe may not be confined to the strict definition of angels, entities such as ministers or messengers.

Who maketh his angels spirits; his ministers a flaming fire (Psalms 104:4) (KJV).

WHY DOES JUDGMENT LINGER?

Lucifer's rebellion would affect some of the assembly, but not all. Its effects would not, however, be seen until the time of the end. God, of course, would and did know in whose being this traitorous act had sunk its deep roots, but this would not be apparent to the other beings of the realm until this traitorous act had run its full course.

Anyone who has done any gardening knows that seedlings look a lot alike before they grow and develop into plants. It is not until they obtain some maturity that they start to visibly differ one from another.

As another example, let us say a man abuses his wife and that he has a child. This child observes this abuse. How will it affect him? Will the effect be seen as he is a child, or will it be years later, when as an adult he is married and has his own wife? The law of averages says he will himself become an abuser.

One might say a seed was planted when he observed the abuse as a child, and later the seed of abuse sprung to full growth when he grew up and took a wife.

Could anyone have looked at the child and known that he would grow up to be an abuser? No, it takes time for this abuse (sin) to mature and to grow to its full-blown proportions.

This is the same[56] principle as has taken place among the beings of the spiritual realm. Observing the traitorous act planted a seed among the beings of the spiritual realm. Only in time would this traitorous act mature and the unaffected spiritual beings of the realm see the effect on those in whom this traitorous act had been allowed to harbor and take root.

Once this traitorous act has run its full course and become manifest in all whom have allowed it to germinate, then Judgment, the End of Days, will occur. Hence, the reason justice has lingered so long. This is why suffering, sin, and misery occur, but it will have its day.

If you have enjoyed this book, or it has had an impact on your life, we would like to hear from you.

CK Quarterman is available to speak at your function, church group, or meeting on any Bible subject.

If you would like CK Quarterman to join your discussion by phone, please include that in your request. He would be more than happy to join you for an hour by conference line.

Appointments will be set on a first come basis, and depend on availability.

Endnotes

PROLOGUE

1   "For yourselves know perfectly that the day of the Lord so cometh as a thief in the night" (1 Thess. 5:2).

2   "When ye therefore shall see the abomination of desolation, spoken of by Daniel the prophet, stand in the holy place, (whoso readeth, let him understand:) Then let them which be in Judaea flee into the mountains: Let him which is on the housetop not come down to take anything out of his house: Neither let him which is in the field return back to take his clothes. And woe unto them that are with child, and to them that give suck in those days! But pray ye that your flight be not in the winter, neither on the sabbath day" (Matt. 24:15-20) (KJV)

3   "Why standest thou afar off, O LORD? why hidest thou thyself in times of trouble?" (Ps. 10:1)

4   Matt. 13:44–49

5   "But the Spirit explicitly says that in later times some will fall away from the faith, paying attention to deceitful spirits and doctrines of demons" (1 Timothy 4:1).

6   "The LORD possessed me in the beginning of his way, before his works of old" (Prov. 8:22).

7   "A horse [is] a vain thing for safety: neither shall he deliver [any] by his great strength" (Psa. 33:7).

THE UNSEEN BATTLE

8   We are told of this unseen battle which rages around us in Paul's letter to the Ephesians. Paul makes this statement: "For we wrestle not against flesh and blood, but against principalities, against powers, against the rulers of the darkness of this world, against spiritual wickedness in high places" (Eph. 6:12). In some modern versions the word rulers is replaced with the word powers. Either way, we get the idea that there are dark rulers behind politicians, and the real forces we face upon the battlefield may be hidden from our eyes.

9   His Christianity is often hotly debated, but he stopped the persecutions under Diocletian and returned the property of Christians that had been confiscated under Diocletian. This supernatural event is documented by his testimony and that of his biographers.

10 AD- Anno Domini is Medieval Latin, and it is translated as "In the year of (the/Our) Lord."

11 Daniel 10:11-16, paraphrased by the author

12 Eons - Eon means "age" or "forever" and in geology, an eon is a large division of time.

13 Ancient of Days - God the Father

TIME BEFORE TIME

14 Everlasting - "The LORD possessed me in the beginning of his way, before his works of old. I was set up from everlasting, from the beginning, or ever the earth was. When there were

no depths, I was brought forth; when there were no fountains abounding with water. Before the mountains were settled, before the hills was I brought forth: While as yet he had not made the earth, nor the fields, nor the highest part of the dust of the world. When he prepared the heavens, I was there: when he set a compass upon the face of the depth: When he established the clouds above: when he strengthened the fountains of the deep: When he gave to the sea his decree, that the waters should not pass his commandment: when he appointed the foundations of the earth: Then I was by him, as one brought up with him: and I was daily his delight, rejoicing always before him; Rejoicing in the habitable part of his earth; and my delights were with the sons of men" (Proverbs 8:22-31).

15 This is the Christian doctrine called ex nihilo. It means to create something out of nothing.

16 Logos – Christ Jesus - Christ is the Logos (λόγος, the Greek for word, wisdom or reason) establishing the doctrine of the divinity of Logos Christ and Logos as revealer of the deus absconditus (the unseen God).

17 "upholding all things by the word of his power" (Heb.1:3)

18 "Through faith we understand that the worlds were framed by the word of God, so that things which are seen were not made of things which do appear" (Heb. 11:3).

19 Job
The time in which Job lived was said by the historian Eusebius to be two ages before Moses, that is, about eighteen hundred years before Christ or six hundred years after the Flood.

20 Job 1:6
"One day the angels came to present themselves before the LORD, and Satan also came with them." (NIV)

"Now there was a day when the sons (the angels) of God came to present themselves before the Lord, and Satan (the adversary and accuser) also came among them." (AMP)

"Now there was a day when the sons of God came to present themselves before the LORD, and Satan came also among them." (KJV)

"Do you listen in on God's council? Do you limit wisdom to yourself?" (Job 15:8)

21 Rev. 4:2–8, paraphrased

22 "Then another angel, having a golden censer, came and stood at the altar. And much incense was given to him, so that he could offer it with the prayers of all the saints upon the golden altar which is before the throne" (Rev. 8:3).

23 See 1 Kings 22:20–22 as it is paraphrased here by the author.

24 1 Kings 22:20–23

And Jehovah said, "Who shall entice Ahab, that he may go up and fall at Ramoth-gilead?" And one said on this manner; and another said on that manner. And there came forth a spirit, and stood before Jehovah, and said, "I will entice him." And Jehovah said to him, "Wherewith?" And he said, "I will go forth, and will be a lying spirit in the mouth of all his prophets." And he said, "Thou shalt entice him, and shalt prevail also: go forth, and do so."

HOW THE CONSPIRACY BEGAN

25 "For the love of money is the root (beginning) of all evil (sin)" (1 Tim. 6:10).

26 Lucifer is Latin and is composed of two words: lux, meaning light, and ferre, which means to bear or to bring. Thus, the name Lucifer means bearer of light.

27 Rahab would also have been visible in the early morning hours from Earth's perspective as Saturn is now. Perhaps this is where Lucifer got the title son of the morning, or bearer of light.

28 "You have broken Rahab in pieces, as one slain: you have scattered your enemies with your mighty arm" (Ps. 89:10) .

29 The Sicilian ethnographer, Giuseppe Pitrè, at the end of the 19th century wrote these words.

30 Eze. 28:13–19

DESOLATE PLANET

31 "The Gap Theory" and "Special Creation" – There are two lines of thought in Christianity today about the event of creation. There are those who believe that God created the world in six days, and others who believe that God created the world in Genesis, but between verses one and two Lucifer rebelled, causing God's judgment upon the Earth as well as Lucifer's realm. The opponents of this view see verse two as God's judgment upon Lucifer, and the Earth as part of Lucifer's realm. This view holds that the six days of God's creation in Genesis is a "remaking process." This view relies heavily upon the Hebrew word "Asah," translated as "made" to mean "to make from pre-existing matter"–that matter of Genesis verse one.

32 Gen. 1:2
    And the earth was void and empty (DRB), Now the earth was unformed and void (JPS), and the earth being without form and empty (LITV), the earth hath existed waste and void (YLT)

33 Dake's Bible points out in the margin that the Earth was not created without form and void. It became without form and void.

34 Jeremiah 4:23–28

35 In essence, what I am saying is this, that Romans 5:12 upon quick observation might seem to rule out the possibility of death in the world before Adam, thereby making a pre-Adamite world an impossibility. However, it states merely that Adam brought sin and death unto himself and his descendants. The Greek word Kosmos, translated as "world" in most Bibles, simply means a social system. As seen in this light, Romans 5:12 is saying that Adam caused sin and death to come upon the world, or social system of humanity. No pre-Adamite world is addressed in these verses, and therefore a pre-Adamite world cannot be ruled out. These verses are merely stating that Adam brought sin and death to humanity.

36 Proposed by Thomas Chalmers (c. 1814) and popularized by G.H. Pember in his 1876 work, Earth's Earliest Ages. The idea of a gap became popular when Finis Jennings Dake included it in his famous work, the Dake Reference Bible.

THE DARK LORDS

37 Enoch 14:2

38 "I was looking in the visions of my head on my bed. And, behold, a watcher, even a holy one, came down from the heaven" (Daniel 4:13).

39 Mt. Hermon derives its name from the Hebrew word herem meaning "a curse."

40 Book of Jubilees 5:5–9

41 Book of Enoch 10:6

42 Book of Enoch 18:16

43 These are verses where Giants or Rephaim, another Hebrew word for Giant, is used in Scripture.

   "There were giants in the earth in those days; and also after that, when the sons of God came in unto the daughters of men, and they bare children to them, the same became mighty men which were of old, men of renown" (Gen. 6:4).

"And there we saw the giants, the sons of Anak, which come of the giants: and we were in our own sight as grasshoppers, and so we were in their sight" (Num. 13:33).

"Which also were accounted giants, as the Anakims; but the Moabites call them Emims" (Deu. 2:11).

"That also was accounted a land of giants: giants dwelt therein in old time; and the Ammonites call them Zamzummims" (Deu. 2:20).

"For only Og king of Bashan remained of the remnant of giants; behold, his bedstead was a bedstead of iron; is it not in Rabbath of the children of Ammon? Nine cubits was the length thereof, and four cubits the breadth of it, after the cubit of a man" (Deu. 3:11).

"And the rest of Gilead, and all Bashan, being the kingdom of Og, gave I unto the half tribe of Manasseh; all the region of Argob, with all Bashan, which was called the land of giants" (Deu. 3:13).

"And the coast of Og king of Bashan, which was of the remnant of the giants, that dwelt at Ashtaroth and at Edrei" (Joshua 12:4).

"All the kingdom of Og in Bashan, which reigned in Ashtaroth and in Edrei, who remained of the remnant of the giants: for these did Moses smite, and cast them out" (Joshua 13:12).

"And the border went up by the valley of the son of Hinnom unto the south side of the Jebusite; the same is Jerusalem: and the border went up to the top of the mountain that lieth before the valley of Hinnom westward, which is at the end of the valley of the giants northward" (Joshua 15:8).

"And Joshua answered them, If thou be a great people, then get thee up to the wood country, and cut down for thyself there in the land of the Perizzites and of the giants, if Mount Ephraim be too narrow for thee" (Joshua 17:15).

"And the border came down to the end of the mountain that lieth before the valley of the son of Hinnom, and which is in the valley of the giants on the north, and descended to the valley of Hinnom, to the side of Jebusi on the south, and descended to Enrogel" (Joshua 18:16).

"And Ishbibenob, which was of the sons of the giant, the weight of whose spear weighed three hundred shekels of brass in weight, he being girded with a new sword, thought to have slain David" (2 Sam. 21:16).

"And it came to pass after this, that there was again a battle with the Philistines at Gob: then Sibbechai the Hushathite slew Saph, which was of the sons of the giant. And there was yet a battle in Gath, where was a man of great stature, that had on every hand six fingers, and on every foot six toes, four and twenty in number; and he also was born to the giant. These four were born to the giant in Gath, and fell by the hand of David, and by the hand of his servant" (2 Sam. 21:18, 20, 22).

"And it came to pass after this, that there arose war at Gezer with the Philistines; at which time Sibbechai the Hushathite slew Sippai, that was of the children of the giant: and they were subdued. And yet again there was war at Gath, where was a man of great stature, whose fingers and toes were four and twenty, six on each hand, and six on each foot: and he also was the son of the giant.. These were born unto the giant in Gath; and they fell by the hand of David, and by the hand of his servants" (1 Chron. 20:4, 6, 8)

"He breaketh me with breach upon breach, he runneth upon me like a giant" (Job 16:14).

"And in the fourteenth year came Chedorlaomer, and the kings that were with him, and smote the Rephaims in Ashteroth Karnaim, and the Zuzims in Ham, and the Emims in Shaveh Kiriathaim" (Gen. 14:5).

"And the Hittites, and the Perizzites, and the Rephaims" (Gen. 15:20).

"The Philistines also came and spread themselves in the valley of Rephaim" (2 Sam. 5:18)

"Dead (Rephaim-Giant) things are formed from under the waters, and the inhabitants thereof" (Job 26:5).

"Hell from beneath is moved for thee to meet thee at thy coming: it stirreth up the dead (Rephaim-Giant) for thee, even all the chief ones of the earth; it hath raised up from their thrones all the kings of the nations" (Isa. 14:9).

"Thy dead men shall live, together with my dead body shall they arise. Awake and sing, ye that dwell in dust: for thy dew is as the dew of herbs, and the earth shall cast out the dead (Rephaim-Giant)" (Isa. 26:19).

44 Dolan, Richard M., UFOs and the National Security State, Keyhole Publishing, 2009, pgs. 322-323

45 Ps. 18:7–15

STARGATES

46 Ps. 18:12

47 Exo. 19:16–20

48 Heb. 12:21

49 Enoch 14:9

CONSPIRACY

50 Matt. 24:38–39 (KJV)

51 Matt. 24:30–31 (KJV)

52 http://www.thebyteshow.com/DouglasRiggs.html   Pastor Douglas Riggs Website

53 These petroglyphs can be seen at New Mexico's official website (http://www.vivanewmexico.com). Also, at the Newspaper Rock area of Utah there are petroglyphs of six-toed feet.

EPILOGUE

54 Revelation of John 6:15:

15 And the kings of the earth, and the great men, and the rich men, and the chief captains, and the mighty men, and every bondman, and every free man, hid themselves in the dens and in the rocks of the mountains;

Revelation of John 6:16:

16 And said to the mountains and rocks, Fall on us, and hide us from the face of him that sitteth on the throne, and from the wrath of the Lamb:

55 EMP - electromagnetic pulse is a burst of electromagnetic radiation resulting from a nuclear explosion at high altitude. In 1962, a 1.44 megaton nuclear missile was detonated in space, 250 miles above the Pacific Ocean, in a test called Starfish Prime. It caused disruption 898 miles away in Hawaii. Russian tests indicate that several high altitude bursts would disable all communications in North America.

56 To see this by example, we must look at Matt.13:36 where the tares and the wheat grow together until the end of the world.

For more information about
CK Quarterman
&
Fallen Angels
please visit:

www.fallenangels-ckquarterman.com
ckquarter@hotmail.com
http://twitter.com/bizckquarter
http://www.facebook.com/ckquarter

For more information about
AMBASSADOR INTERNATIONAL
please visit:

www.ambassador-international.com
@AmbassadorIntl
www.facebook.com/AmbassadorIntl